JavaScript for Beginners Who Hate Boring Handbooks

Learn by Doing: Build Interactive Sites and Projects with Confidence

Booker Blunt

Rafael Sanders

Miguel Farmer

Boozman Richard

All rights reserved

How to Scan a Barcode to Get a Repository

1. **Install a QR/Barcode Scanner** – Ensure you have a barcode or QR code scanner app installed on your smartphone or use a built-in scanner in **GitHub, GitLab, or Bitbucket.**

2. **Open the Scanner** – Launch the scanner app and grant necessary camera permissions.

3. **Scan the Barcode** – Align the barcode within the scanning frame. The scanner will automatically detect and process it.

4. **Follow the Link** – The scanned result will display a **URL to the repository**. Tap the link to open it in your web browser or Git client.

5. **Clone the Repository** – Use **Git clone** with the provided URL to download the repository to your local machine.

Chapter 1: Setting Up Your JavaScript Workshop

In this chapter, we're going to lay the foundation for your JavaScript journey. You'll get your development environment set up with all the tools you need to start coding right away. We'll install the key software like **VS Code, Node.js,** and **npm,** and we'll familiarize ourselves with Chrome's built-in developer tools, which will become indispensable as you start writing and debugging your code.

Before diving into the code itself, let's talk about what a "workshop" really means in the context of programming. In this case, your workshop is where you'll spend your time building, testing, and debugging your JavaScript projects. It's not just about the software; it's also about the environment you create for yourself. A well-organized workspace can make a huge difference in your productivity. So, let's start by setting up everything you need to make your development experience as smooth and efficient as possible.

Installing VS Code: The Heart of Your Coding Environment

Visual Studio Code (VS Code) is the most popular code editor among developers, and for a good reason. It's lightweight, yet powerful, and it's packed with features that make writing and debugging JavaScript a breeze. To install VS Code, you'll need to download it from the official website.

Go to Visual Studio Code and hit the download button for your operating system (Windows, macOS, or Linux). The installation process is straightforward, but there are a few things to note along the way. Make sure you select the options to add VS Code to your system PATH and integrate it with your file explorer. These simple steps will save you time in the future when you're running your projects directly from VS Code or the command line.

Once installed, launch VS Code and take a moment to familiarize yourself with the layout. The left sidebar is where you'll navigate your project files, the central area is where you'll write your code, and the bottom panel is where you'll see the output, errors, and logs of your projects. The right-hand side will eventually house any extensions you install, and there's a lot to explore in that section. For now, we'll keep it simple.

Installing Node.js and npm: Your JavaScript Powerhouse

Next up is installing **Node.js** and **npm**. While JavaScript is commonly used for frontend development in the browser, Node.js allows you to run JavaScript on the server-side as well, making JavaScript a versatile language for both ends of web development. npm (Node Package Manager) is included with Node.js, and it's an essential tool for managing and installing JavaScript libraries and frameworks that you'll use in your projects.

To get started, go to the official Node.js website at Node.js and download the latest LTS version (the Long-Term Support version). The installation process is similar to that of VS Code, and it will also include npm.

Once Node.js is installed, it's time to verify the installation. Open up your terminal (or command prompt on Windows), and type the following commands:

```
nginx

node -v
npm -v
```

These commands will output the current versions of Node.js and npm installed on your system. If you see version numbers, congratulations! You're ready to start building with JavaScript. If not, go back and troubleshoot the installation process to ensure everything is set up correctly.

Familiarizing Yourself with Chrome DevTools

Now that you have the basic tools in place, let's take a closer look at **Chrome Developer Tools** (DevTools). These tools are built into Google Chrome and are incredibly useful for testing, debugging, and inspecting the HTML, CSS, and JavaScript of any website you visit. As a developer, you'll be spending a lot of time in DevTools, so it's important to understand how to use them effectively.

To access DevTools, simply open Google Chrome, right-click anywhere on a web page, and select **Inspect** or press `Ctrl + Shift + I` on Windows or `Cmd + Option + I` on macOS. This will open up the DevTools window, usually at the bottom of your browser.

The **Console** tab is where you'll see log messages, errors, and output from your JavaScript code. You can also run JavaScript commands directly in the Console. For example, try typing:

```cpp
console.log("Hello, Team!");
```

You'll see the message appear in the console. This is a simple example, but it's a good starting point for debugging. Any errors in your code will also appear here, and it's essential to get comfortable with reading these error messages.

The **Elements** tab lets you inspect the structure of the webpage. You can view and modify the HTML and CSS of the page in real time. This is useful for tweaking your project's design or checking for issues with your HTML structure.

As we move forward with building our first project, we'll return to DevTools to troubleshoot and refine our code, so getting comfortable here early on will pay off in the long run.

Creating Your First JavaScript Project: The "Hello, Team!" Page

Now that you've set up your development environment and explored the basic tools, it's time to get your hands dirty with some real code.

We'll start with a simple project: a "Hello, Team!" page that greets the user by name.

Let's break this down step by step:

1. **Create a New Project Folder**: Start by creating a folder on your computer where you'll store all your project files. You can name it something like `hello-team` or anything that makes sense to you.

2. **Open VS Code**: Launch VS Code and go to **File > Open Folder** to open your project folder. You'll see an empty workspace where you can begin creating files.

3. **Create the HTML File**: Inside your project folder, create a new file called `index.html`. This will be the HTML file that holds the structure of your webpage. Open the file and add the following code:

```html
<!DOCTYPE html>
<html lang="en">
<head>
    <meta charset="UTF-8">
    <meta name="viewport" content="width=device-width, initial-scale=1.0">
    <title>Hello, Team!</title>
</head>
```

```
<body>
    <h1>Hello, Team!</h1>
    <p id="greeting"></p>

    <script src="app.js"></script>
</body>
</html>
```

This HTML file sets up a basic structure with a heading that says "Hello, Team!" and a paragraph that will later display a personalized greeting.

4. **Create the JavaScript File**: Now, let's create the JavaScript file that will handle the greeting. In the same project folder, create a file named `app.js`. Open it and add the following code:

```javascript
const userName = prompt("What is your name?");
document.getElementById("greeting").innerText =
`Hello, ${userName}! Welcome to the team.`;
```

This JavaScript code prompts the user for their name and then updates the paragraph with an ID of `greeting` to say, "Hello, [name]! Welcome to the team."

5. **Test Your Project**: Now, open the `index.html` file in Chrome. You should see the page with the heading "Hello, Team!" and a prompt asking for your name. Once you enter your name, the greeting will appear below the heading.

If the greeting doesn't appear or you get an error, head back to the **Console** tab in DevTools and check for any issues. You might see an error message like "Uncaught TypeError: Cannot read property 'innerText' of null," which would indicate a problem with the `getElementById` call. This can happen if the JavaScript runs before the HTML is fully loaded, but we'll cover fixes for these kinds of issues in later chapters.

Key Takeaways

By the end of this chapter, you've learned how to set up your coding environment and run your first JavaScript project. You've installed VS Code, Node.js, and npm, and you've learned how to navigate Chrome DevTools for debugging. You've also written a simple JavaScript program that interacts with the user and updates the page dynamically.

This is just the beginning of your JavaScript journey, and as you move forward, you'll gain more confidence in your ability to write interactive web applications. The key here is practice: keep experimenting with small projects and challenges, and soon you'll be building more complex and exciting applications.

Chapter 2: Managing Data — Types and Structures

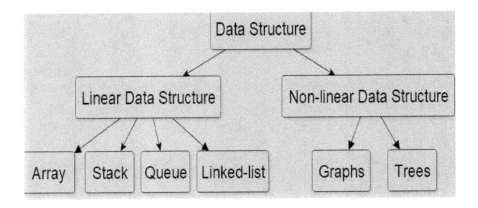

In the world of programming, data is everything. It's the building block of all the applications you'll build. Understanding how to work with data is a critical skill, especially when you're learning JavaScript. Whether you're building a simple app or designing a complex system, you'll always be manipulating data in one form or another. In this chapter, we're going to explore how JavaScript handles data through its various types and structures. We'll break down the core concepts of strings, numbers, booleans, arrays, objects, and maps, and show you how to work with them in real-world scenarios.

We will also dive into how you can store, access, and manipulate these data types efficiently. As a practical exercise, we'll build a tiny inventory tracker that will allow you to add, edit, and list items—one of the most common tasks in software development. By the end of this chapter, you'll understand the underlying data structures in JavaScript and how to apply them in your projects.

Understanding Data Types in JavaScript

Before you can effectively work with data in JavaScript, it's essential to know the various data types the language offers. Each data type serves a specific purpose and behaves differently, so understanding the nuances of each is vital.

1. Strings

Strings are one of the most common data types in any programming language. In JavaScript, strings are used to store and manipulate text. You can create a string by enclosing characters within single quotes ('), double quotes ("), or backticks (`).

Here's an example:

```javascript
let firstName = "John";
let lastName = 'Doe';
let greeting = `Hello, ${firstName} ${lastName}!`;
```

```
console.log(greeting);   // Output: Hello, John Doe!
```

Strings can be concatenated, which means you can join multiple strings together using the + operator, or use template literals (backticks) for cleaner and more readable code.

Strings also come with a variety of built-in methods that allow you to manipulate them. For example, you can get the length of a string with .length, or convert it to uppercase with .toUpperCase():

```javascript
let message = "hello world";
console.log(message.length);         // Output: 11
console.log(message.toUpperCase()); // Output: HELLO
WORLD
```

Understanding how to use strings and their methods is essential because text-based data is involved in nearly every application.

2. Numbers

Numbers in JavaScript are used for mathematical operations, like addition, subtraction, multiplication, and division. JavaScript only has one type of number: the Number type, which can represent both integer and floating-point numbers.

For example:

```javascript
let integer = 42;
let floatingPoint = 3.14;
let sum = integer + floatingPoint;
console.log(sum);   // Output: 45.14
```

Numbers also have special properties like NaN (Not a Number) for invalid operations, and Infinity for values that are too large to represent.

```javascript
let invalidOperation = 0 / 0;
console.log(invalidOperation);   // Output: NaN

let largeNumber = 1e1000;
console.log(largeNumber); // Output: Infinity
```

When working with numbers, you need to be mindful of rounding errors, especially with floating-point numbers.

3. Booleans

A boolean represents a logical value: either true or false. They are incredibly useful for control flow in programming, such as in conditional statements (e.g., if/else), and are used extensively for validation and decision-making processes.

For instance:

```javascript

let isAdmin = true;
let isActive = false;

if (isAdmin) {
  console.log("Welcome, Admin!");
} else {
  console.log("Access Denied.");
}
```

Booleans are often the result of comparisons, like checking if two values are equal or greater than a certain number.

```javascript

let isEqual = (5 === 5);  // true
let isGreater = (10 > 5); // true
```

4. Arrays

Arrays are one of the most powerful data structures in JavaScript. They allow you to store multiple values in a single variable. Arrays can hold elements of any type, including strings, numbers, booleans, and even other arrays or objects.

Here's how you create an array:

```javascript
let fruits = ['Apple', 'Banana', 'Orange'];
console.log(fruits[0]); // Output: Apple
```

Arrays are zero-indexed, meaning the first element is at index 0, the second element is at index 1, and so on. You can also use various array methods to manipulate the elements:

```javascript
fruits.push('Grapes');   // Adds 'Grapes' to the end
fruits.pop();            // Removes the last element
fruits.shift();          // Removes the first element
```

Arrays are especially useful for storing lists, and you'll find them invaluable when you need to handle multiple data items simultaneously.

5. Objects

Objects in JavaScript are key-value pairs that allow you to store more complex data structures. Unlike arrays, which store data in a linear fashion, objects store data in an unordered collection of key-value pairs. Each key in an object is a string (or symbol), and each value can be any data type.

Here's an example of how to create an object:

javascript

```
let person = {
  name: 'Alice',
  age: 30,
  isActive: true
};
```

You access the values of an object using either dot notation (`person.name`) or bracket notation (`person['name']`):

javascript

```
console.log(person.name);   // Output: Alice
```

Objects are essential for modeling more complex data, like users, products, or orders in an e-commerce app.

6. Maps

Maps are similar to objects, but they allow for more flexibility. In JavaScript, objects can only have strings or symbols as keys, whereas maps can have any data type as a key, including objects, functions, or any primitive value.

```javascript
let map = new Map();
map.set('name', 'Bob');
map.set(1, 'Number One');
console.log(map.get('name'));   // Output: Bob
```

Maps are especially useful when you need to store key-value pairs where the keys can be of any type or need to preserve the order of insertion.

Building the Inventory Tracker Project

Now that we have a solid understanding of JavaScript's data types, let's apply our knowledge in a practical project: building a **Tiny Inventory Tracker**. The goal is to create a simple application that allows us to add, edit, and list items in a small warehouse inventory. This is a very common use case in real-world applications like inventory management systems.

Step 1: Defining the Inventory Structure

To start, we need a structure to hold our inventory. An inventory can be represented as an array of objects. Each object will represent an item, and it will contain several properties like `id`, `name`, `quantity`, and `price`.

```javascript
let inventory = [
    { id: 1, name: 'Laptop', quantity: 10, price: 1200 },
    { id: 2, name: 'Phone', quantity: 25, price: 800 }
];
```

Step 2: Adding Items to the Inventory

We'll create a function that adds new items to our inventory. This function will take in the item details (name, quantity, and price), generate a unique ID, and then push the new item into the `inventory` array.

```javascript
function addItem(name, quantity, price) {
    let id = inventory.length + 1;
    inventory.push({ id, name, quantity, price });
}
```

Step 3: Editing Items in the Inventory

Next, we'll need a function to edit an item's details. The function will take the item's `id` and the new details, and it will update the corresponding item in the `inventory`.

javascript

```
function editItem(id, newName, newQuantity, newPrice)
{
   let item = inventory.find(i => i.id === id);
   if (item) {
     item.name = newName;
     item.quantity = newQuantity;
     item.price = newPrice;
   }
}
```

Step 4: Listing Inventory Items

Finally, we need a way to list all items in our inventory. We'll create a function that loops through the `inventory` array and logs each item's details to the console.

javascript

```
function listInventory() {
   inventory.forEach(item => {
```

```
    console.log(`ID: ${item.id}, Name: ${item.name},
Quantity: ${item.quantity}, Price: $${item.price}`);
  });
}
```

Step 5: Putting It All Together

Now, let's test our functions:

```
javascript
```

```
addItem('Tablet', 15, 500);
editItem(2, 'Smartphone', 30, 750);
listInventory();
```

After running this code, you should see the updated inventory, including the new item and the edited item.

Key Takeaways

In this chapter, you've learned how to work with JavaScript's core data types and structures: strings, numbers, booleans, arrays, objects, and maps. You've also learned how to apply these data types to a real-world project—a simple inventory tracker. Understanding how to store and manipulate data in different forms is essential for building effective applications. As you move forward, you'll encounter even more advanced data structures and concepts, but the foundation laid in this chapter will serve you well.

By the end of this chapter, you should feel confident handling different types of data and organizing it effectively within your JavaScript applications. This is a crucial skill, and it's one that you'll rely on again and again as you build more complex projects. So keep practicing, and don't be afraid to experiment with different data structures to see what works best for your specific needs.

Chapter 3: Steering Logic — Conditions and Loops

One of the fundamental skills you'll need as a programmer is the ability to control the flow of your program. You've already seen how data flows through your code, but how do you decide what to do with that data? How do you make decisions based on input or conditions? And how do you repeat tasks multiple times efficiently? This is where conditions and loops come into play.

In this chapter, we'll explore the core control structures in JavaScript that allow you to steer the logic of your programs: `if/else`, `switch`, `for`, `while`, and `forEach` loops. These are the tools you'll use to make decisions and repeat tasks based on specific criteria.

We'll apply what we learn by creating a shipping cost calculator—an app that calculates shipping costs based on different factors, such as weight, distance, and delivery speed. This project will allow you to practice all of the key concepts in this chapter in a practical, real-world scenario.

By the end of this chapter, you'll be comfortable working with conditions and loops in JavaScript. You'll understand how to use them to handle decision-making and repetitive tasks, and you'll have developed a deeper understanding of how to write clean, efficient, and readable code.

Understanding Conditions in JavaScript

In programming, conditions allow you to make decisions based on certain criteria. For example, "If the user is logged in, show the dashboard; otherwise, show the login screen." In JavaScript, we use conditional statements such as `if`, `else if`, and `else` to make these decisions.

1. The `if` Statement

The `if` statement is the most basic form of conditional logic. It tests a condition, and if that condition evaluates to `true`, it runs the code inside the block. If the condition is `false`, it skips over the code block.

Here's a simple example:

```javascript
let userAge = 20;

if (userAge >= 18) {
    console.log("You are an adult.");
```

```
}
```

In this example, we're checking if the `userAge` is greater than or equal to 18. If it is, the program prints "You are an adult." If `userAge` is less than 18, nothing happens.

2. The `else` Statement

Sometimes, you want to do one thing if the condition is true and something else if the condition is false. This is where the `else` statement comes in.

javascript

```javascript
let userAge = 16;

if (userAge >= 18) {
    console.log("You are an adult.");
} else {
    console.log("You are a minor.");
}
```

In this case, if the `userAge` is less than 18, the program will print "You are a minor."

3. The `else if` Statement

You can also chain multiple conditions together using `else if`. This allows you to test multiple conditions in sequence.

```javascript
let userAge = 25;

if (userAge < 13) {
    console.log("You are a child.");
} else if (userAge >= 13 && userAge < 18) {
    console.log("You are a teenager.");
} else {
    console.log("You are an adult.");
}
```

Here, the program first checks if the user is a child (under 13), then checks if they are a teenager (13-17), and if neither condition is true, it defaults to the adult category.

4. Truthy and Falsy Values

In JavaScript, conditions rely on **truthy** and **falsy** values. A **truthy** value evaluates to `true`, and a **falsy** value evaluates to `false`. Some examples of falsy values include `false`, 0, " " (empty string), `null`, `undefined`, and `NaN`. Everything else is considered truthy.

For example:

```javascript

let value = 0;

if (value) {
    console.log("This will not run because 0 is
falsy.");
} else {
    console.log("This will run because 0 is falsy.");
}
```

Understanding Loops in JavaScript

While conditions help you make decisions, loops allow you to repeat actions. Loops are essential when you need to perform the same task multiple times, such as iterating over an array of items or processing multiple records in a database.

1. The `for` Loop

The `for` loop is one of the most commonly used loops in JavaScript. It's great for situations where you know how many times you need to iterate, like iterating over an array of known length.

The basic structure of a `for` loop looks like this:

```javascript
for (let i = 0; i < 5; i++) {
    console.log(i);
}
```

Here's how it works:

- **Initialization**: `let i = 0;` — This initializes the counter variable.
- **Condition**: `i < 5;` — The loop continues running as long as `i` is less than 5.
- **Iteration**: `i++` — After each loop, the counter variable is incremented by 1.

This loop will print the numbers from `0` to `4`.

2. The `while` Loop

A `while` loop runs as long as the specified condition is true. It's useful when you don't know in advance how many iterations you need, but you want to keep looping until a condition is met.

```javascript
let count = 0;

while (count < 5) {
```

```
    console.log(count);
    count++;
}
```

In this case, the loop will keep running until `count` is no longer less than 5.

3. The `do...while` Loop

The `do...while` loop is similar to the `while` loop, except that the code block will always run at least once, even if the condition is false. This is because the condition is evaluated after the code block is executed.

javascript

```
let count = 0;

do {
    console.log(count);
    count++;
} while (count < 5);
```

This loop will also print the numbers from 0 to 4, but it guarantees that the code inside the loop runs at least once.

4. The *forEach* Loop

The forEach method is used for iterating over arrays. It is a cleaner alternative to the traditional for loop when you want to iterate over each element in an array without manually managing the index.

```javascript
let fruits = ['Apple', 'Banana', 'Orange'];

fruits.forEach(function(fruit) {
    console.log(fruit);
});
```

This will print each fruit in the array. Unlike the for loop, you don't need to worry about the index or length of the array—forEach handles that for you.

Applying Logic and Loops to the Shipping Cost Calculator

Now that you understand how conditions and loops work, let's apply them to a real-world problem. We'll build a simple shipping cost calculator that calculates the shipping cost for a package based on its weight, distance, and delivery speed.

We'll use different conditions to decide the cost and loops to calculate the total cost when there are multiple packages to ship.

Step 1: Defining the Shipping Rates

Let's start by defining the basic parameters of our shipping rates. We'll need a set of rules to decide the shipping cost:

- Shipping costs $5 per kilogram of weight.
- If the distance is over 500 km, add an additional $10 for long-distance shipping.
- If the delivery speed is "express," add $20 to the total cost.

javascript

```javascript
function calculateShippingCost(weight, distance,
speed) {
    let cost = weight * 5; // Base cost per kilogram
    if (distance > 500) {
        cost += 10; // Add charge for long-distance
shipping
    }
    if (speed === "express") {
        cost += 20; // Add charge for express
delivery
    }
    return cost;
}
```

In this function:

- We first calculate the base cost by multiplying the weight by $5 per kilogram.
- Then, we check if the distance is over 500 km. If it is, we add $10 to the cost.
- Finally, we check if the delivery speed is "express" and add $20 if it is.

Step 2: Handling Multiple Packages

Now, let's extend this logic to handle multiple packages. We'll create an array of packages, and for each package, we'll calculate the shipping cost using the `calculateShippingCost` function.

javascript

```
let packages = [
    { weight: 10, distance: 300, speed: "standard" },
    { weight: 5, distance: 600, speed: "express" },
    { weight: 15, distance: 150, speed: "standard" }
];

packages.forEach(function(pkg) {
    let cost = calculateShippingCost(pkg.weight,
pkg.distance, pkg.speed);
    console.log(`Shipping cost for package with
weight ${pkg.weight}kg: $${cost}`);
```

```
});
```

Here, we use the `forEach` loop to iterate through the `packages` array. For each package, we call the `calculateShippingCost` function and print out the result.

Step 3: Final Thoughts

By the end of this project, you've applied **conditions** and **loops** to calculate shipping costs based on various criteria. You've learned how to create decision-making logic with `if/else` statements, how to loop through collections of data with `for`, `while`, and `forEach`, and how to organize your code for efficiency.

This chapter has equipped you with the skills to make your programs dynamic and responsive to different situations. As you continue building with JavaScript, you'll find that conditions and loops are among the most commonly used tools in your toolkit, and mastering them will make you a much more capable developer.

Chapter 4: Organizing Code with Functions

As you dive deeper into JavaScript, one of the most crucial concepts you'll need to master is organizing your code using functions. Functions are the backbone of writing clean, reusable, and efficient code. They allow you to break down complex problems into smaller, manageable chunks and perform repetitive tasks without duplicating code. As your projects grow, you'll find yourself using functions more and more to ensure your code stays organized and scalable.

In this chapter, we're going to explore how to define and use functions in JavaScript. We'll cover the basic syntax, how to handle parameters and return values, and dive into more advanced topics like Immediately Invoked Function Expressions (IIFE) and the popular arrow function syntax. We'll also work through a practical example— a multi-unit converter that handles temperature, weight, and length conversions.

By the end of this chapter, you'll have a solid understanding of how to use functions to organize your code and make it more reusable. You'll also learn the principles of writing functions that are easy to maintain, debug, and extend.

The Basics of Functions

A function in JavaScript is essentially a block of reusable code designed to perform a specific task. It can take inputs, process them, and return a result. Functions help you keep your code **DRY**—Don't Repeat Yourself—by allowing you to write a piece of code once and use it as many times as needed.

1. Defining a Function

A basic function is defined using the `function` keyword, followed by the function name, parentheses, and curly braces. Inside the parentheses, you can list the parameters that the function will use, and inside the curly braces, you define the code that the function will execute.

Here's a simple function that greets the user:

```javascript
function greetUser() {
    console.log("Hello, welcome to the site!");
}
```

To call or invoke the function, you simply use the function name followed by parentheses:

```javascript
```

```javascript
greetUser();  // Output: Hello, welcome to the site!
```

This function doesn't take any parameters and doesn't return any value—it just logs a message to the console.

2. Parameters and Arguments

In JavaScript, functions can take **parameters**, which are placeholders for the values you want to pass into the function when you call it. When you call the function, you provide the **arguments** that correspond to these parameters.

Here's an example of a function that takes parameters:

```javascript
```

```javascript
function greetUser(name) {
    console.log(`Hello, ${name}! Welcome to the
site.`);
}

greetUser("Alice");  // Output: Hello, Alice! Welcome
to the site.
greetUser("Bob");    // Output: Hello, Bob! Welcome
to the site.
```

In this example, the function `greetUser` takes one parameter, `name`, and uses it to personalize the greeting. When calling the function, you provide different values (arguments) for the `name` parameter.

3. Returning Values from Functions

Functions don't have to just perform actions; they can also **return** values. This means the function can compute something and send the result back to the caller. You can use the `return` keyword to specify what value the function should return.

Here's an example of a function that returns a value:

```javascript
javascript

function addNumbers(a, b) {
    return a + b;
}

let result = addNumbers(5, 7);
console.log(result);   // Output: 12
```

In this example, the `addNumbers` function takes two parameters, `a` and `b`, adds them together, and returns the sum. The returned value is stored in the `result` variable, which is then logged to the console.

4. Scope in Functions

In JavaScript, **scope** refers to the visibility or accessibility of variables in different parts of your code. Functions create their own **local scope**, meaning variables declared inside a function are only accessible within that function, and they don't affect variables outside it.

javascript

```javascript
function example() {
    let localVar = "I am local";
    console.log(localVar);   // Output: I am local
}

example();
console.log(localVar);   // Error: localVar is not
defined
```

Here, `localVar` is only accessible inside the `example` function. If you try to access it outside the function, JavaScript will throw an error because it's out of scope.

On the other hand, **global variables** are accessible anywhere in your code:

```javascript

let globalVar = "I am global";

function example() {
    console.log(globalVar);   // Output: I am global
}

example();
console.log(globalVar);   // Output: I am global
```

While using global variables might seem convenient, it's generally a good idea to avoid them as much as possible, since they can make your code harder to maintain and debug.

Advanced Function Concepts

Once you understand the basics of functions, you can move on to more advanced concepts that will help you write cleaner, more efficient code.

1. *Immediately Invoked Function Expressions (IIFE)*

An **Immediately Invoked Function Expression (IIFE)** is a function that is defined and executed right away. This is useful for creating a function scope to avoid polluting the global namespace, and for organizing code that you want to execute immediately.

Here's how to write an IIFE:

```javascript

(function() {
    console.log("This is an IIFE!");
})();
```

Notice that the function is wrapped in parentheses. This makes it an expression, and by adding `()`, we immediately invoke the function.

IIFEs are commonly used in JavaScript to encapsulate code and avoid potential conflicts with global variables. They're also useful for managing initialization logic when working with modules or libraries.

2. Arrow Functions

Arrow functions are a more concise way to write functions. They use a different syntax than traditional functions and have some important differences in behavior, especially with respect to how they handle `this`.

Here's the syntax for an arrow function:

```javascript

const greetUser = (name) => {
    console.log(`Hello, ${name}!`);
};


greetUser("Alice");   // Output: Hello, Alice!
```

If the function has only one parameter, you can omit the parentheses:

```javascript

const greetUser = name => {
    console.log(`Hello, ${name}!`);
};
```

Arrow functions are not just syntactically shorter—they also behave differently when it comes to the this keyword. Arrow functions don't have their own this context; instead, they inherit this from the surrounding code. This can be extremely useful in certain scenarios, such as inside event handlers or callbacks, where you want to preserve the context of this.

Practical Example: Multi-Unit Converter

Now that you've mastered the basics and advanced concepts of functions, let's apply what you've learned in a practical project: creating a **multi-unit converter**. This simple application will allow users to convert between different units of temperature, weight, and length. The project will give you hands-on experience with defining functions, passing parameters, and returning values.

Step 1: Defining Conversion Functions

We'll start by writing separate functions for converting temperature, weight, and length. Each function will take a value and a unit to convert from, and return the converted value.

Temperature Conversion:

```javascript
function convertTemperature(value, fromUnit, toUnit)
{
    if (fromUnit === "Celsius" && toUnit ===
"Fahrenheit") {
        return value * 9/5 + 32;
    } else if (fromUnit === "Fahrenheit" && toUnit
=== "Celsius") {
        return (value - 32) * 5/9;
    } else {
```

```
        return "Unsupported conversion";
    }
}
```

Weight Conversion:

javascript

```
function convertWeight(value, fromUnit, toUnit) {
    if (fromUnit === "Kilograms" && toUnit ===
"Pounds") {
        return value * 2.20462;
    } else if (fromUnit === "Pounds" && toUnit ===
"Kilograms") {
        return value / 2.20462;
    } else {
        return "Unsupported conversion";
    }
}
```

Length Conversion:

javascript

```
function convertLength(value, fromUnit, toUnit) {
    if (fromUnit === "Meters" && toUnit === "Feet") {
        return value * 3.28084;
    } else if (fromUnit === "Feet" && toUnit ===
"Meters") {
        return value / 3.28084;
```

```
    } else {
        return "Unsupported conversion";
    }
}
```

Step 2: Creating a Converter Function

Next, let's create a single function that uses the above conversion functions for each unit type. This will make the process of converting between units much more streamlined.

javascript

```
function convertUnits(value, fromUnit, toUnit) {
    if (["Celsius", "Fahrenheit"].includes(fromUnit)
&& ["Celsius", "Fahrenheit"].includes(toUnit)) {
        return convertTemperature(value, fromUnit,
toUnit);
    } else if (["Kilograms",
"Pounds"].includes(fromUnit) && ["Kilograms",
"Pounds"].includes(toUnit)) {
        return convertWeight(value, fromUnit,
toUnit);
    } else if (["Meters", "Feet"].includes(fromUnit)
&& ["Meters", "Feet"].includes(toUnit)) {
        return convertLength(value, fromUnit,
toUnit);
    } else {
        return "Invalid units";
    }
```

```
}
```

This `convertUnits` function checks the type of units and calls the appropriate conversion function.

Step 3: Implementing the Converter

To make this project interactive, let's implement a simple user interface. We can create a form with dropdowns for selecting the units and an input field for entering the value to convert.

html

```html
<form id="converterForm">
    <input type="number" id="value"
placeholder="Enter value" required>
    <select id="fromUnit">
        <option value="Celsius">Celsius</option>
        <option
value="Fahrenheit">Fahrenheit</option>
        <option value="Kilograms">Kilograms</option>
        <option value="Pounds">Pounds</option>
        <option value="Meters">Meters</option>
        <option value="Feet">Feet</option>
    </select>
    <select id="toUnit">
        <option value="Celsius">Celsius</option>
        <option
value="Fahrenheit">Fahrenheit</option>
```

```html
        <option value="Kilograms">Kilograms</option>
        <option value="Pounds">Pounds</option>
        <option value="Meters">Meters</option>
        <option value="Feet">Feet</option>
    </select>
    <button type="submit">Convert</button>
</form>
<p id="result"></p>

<script>
document.getElementById("converterForm").addEventList
ener("submit", function(event) {
    event.preventDefault();
    let value =
parseFloat(document.getElementById("value").value);
    let fromUnit =
document.getElementById("fromUnit").value;
    let toUnit =
document.getElementById("toUnit").value;

    let result = convertUnits(value, fromUnit,
toUnit);
    document.getElementById("result").innerText =
`Converted value: ${result}`;
});
</script>
```

Key Takeaways

By the end of this chapter, you've learned how to:

- Define reusable functions to organize your code and keep it clean and DRY.
- Work with parameters and return values to make your functions more flexible and dynamic.
- Implement advanced concepts like Immediately Invoked Function Expressions (IIFE) and arrow functions.
- Apply functions to a practical project, such as creating a multi-unit converter that can be used on any page.

Understanding how to use functions efficiently is a game-changer when it comes to building complex applications. You'll find that functions not only make your code more organized but also help you avoid duplication, which makes your projects easier to maintain and debug.

Chapter 5: Bringing Pages to Life — DOM Manipulation

One of the most powerful aspects of JavaScript is its ability to manipulate the **Document Object Model (DOM)**. The DOM represents the structure of a webpage as a tree of objects, where each element, attribute, and piece of text is an object that can be modified. This chapter will introduce you to the world of DOM manipulation—an essential skill for any web developer. You'll learn how to access and modify the elements of a webpage, update their content dynamically, and create a more interactive user experience.

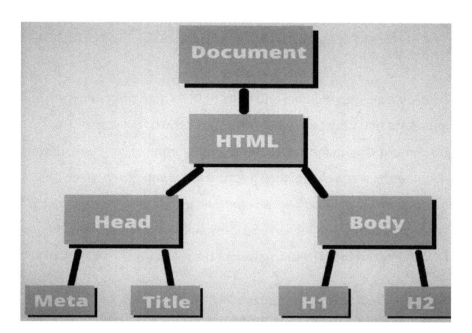

In this chapter, we'll focus on key aspects of DOM manipulation: querying elements, creating new ones, updating their content, and removing them from the page. Additionally, we will create a practical, hands-on project: a live dashboard that simulates real-time sensor readings for a production line. This dashboard will dynamically update its content and give you an understanding of how to work with the DOM in real-time applications.

By the end of this chapter, you'll be comfortable with accessing and manipulating DOM elements, creating interactive and dynamic user interfaces, and understanding the flow of document objects in JavaScript.

Understanding the DOM

Before we get into the nuts and bolts of DOM manipulation, it's important to understand what the DOM is and how it works. The **Document Object Model (DOM)** is a programming interface for web documents. It represents the structure of a webpage as a tree of objects, where each node is an element, attribute, or piece of text. When you load a webpage in your browser, the browser creates a DOM based on the HTML structure of the page.

For example, consider the following HTML:

html

```
<!DOCTYPE html>
<html>
<head>
    <title>DOM Manipulation</title>
</head>
<body>
    <h1>Production Line Dashboard</h1>
    <div id="sensor-readings">
        <p>Temperature: <span
id="temperature">20°C</span></p>
        <p>Pressure: <span id="pressure">1013
hPa</span></p>
        <p>Speed: <span id="speed">0 rpm</span></p>
    </div>
</body>
</html>
```

In the DOM, this HTML structure is represented as a tree:

- The root element is `<html>`.
- The `<head>` and `<body>` elements are child nodes of `<html>`.
- Inside `<body>`, we have the `<h1>` element and the `<div>` element with an ID of `sensor-readings`.
- Inside the `sensor-readings` `<div>`, there are three `<p>` tags, each containing a `<span>` tag.

The DOM allows us to interact with all these elements programmatically. JavaScript can modify the content, style, and even the structure of the document.

Querying Elements in the DOM

The first step in manipulating the DOM is **querying** or selecting elements. JavaScript provides several methods for finding elements on a webpage. The most commonly used methods are `getElementById()`, `getElementsByClassName()`, `getElementsByTagName()`, and `querySelector()`.

1. getElementById()

This method allows you to select an element by its **ID**. Since IDs are supposed to be unique, `getElementById()` will always return only one element.

```javascript
let heading = document.getElementById("sensor-
readings");
console.log(heading);
```

This will return the element with the ID `sensor-readings`.

2. getElementsByClassName()

If you want to select elements by their **class name**, you can use getElementsByClassName(). This returns a live HTMLCollection, meaning that if the DOM is updated, the collection will automatically update as well.

javascript

```
let paragraphs =
document.getElementsByClassName("sensor");
console.log(paragraphs);
```

This will return all elements with the class sensor.

3. getElementsByTagName()

Similarly, you can select elements by their **tag name** using getElementsByTagName(). This also returns an HTMLCollection.

javascript

```
let allParagraphs =
document.getElementsByTagName("p");
console.log(allParagraphs);
```

This will return all <p> elements in the document.

4. querySelector ()

For more complex queries, `querySelector()` is a powerful method. It allows you to select elements using **CSS selectors**.

```javascript
javascript

let temperature =
document.querySelector("#temperature");
console.log(temperature);
```

This will return the element with the ID `temperature`. `querySelector()` can also be used to select the first element that matches a CSS selector.

5. querySelectorAll ()

If you want to select **multiple elements** that match a CSS selector, you can use `querySelectorAll()`. This returns a **NodeList** (not an HTMLCollection), which is static and does not update automatically when the DOM changes.

```javascript
javascript

let sensorReadings =
document.querySelectorAll(".sensor");
console.log(sensorReadings);
```

This will return a NodeList of all elements with the class `sensor`.

Modifying the DOM: Creating, Updating, and Removing Elements

Once you've queried elements from the DOM, you'll want to modify them. JavaScript provides various ways to interact with and update DOM elements, such as changing their content, updating their styles, and adding or removing child elements.

1. Updating Element Content

To change the content of an element, you can use the `.textContent` or `.innerHTML` properties. Use `.textContent` when you want to modify plain text, and `.innerHTML` when you want to update HTML content.

```javascript
```

```javascript
let temperature =
document.getElementById("temperature");
temperature.textContent = "22°C";  // Updates the
text inside the span
```
```javascript
```

```
let sensorReadings = document.getElementById("sensor-
readings");
sensorReadings.innerHTML = "<p>New sensor
readings...</p>";  // Replaces the content inside the
div
```

2. Updating Styles

To update an element's style, you can use the `.style` property. This allows you to change inline styles directly with JavaScript.

```javascript
let sensorReadings = document.getElementById("sensor-
readings");
sensorReadings.style.backgroundColor = "lightgreen";
```

You can also modify other styles like font size, color, width, height, etc.

3. Adding and Removing Elements

You can dynamically create new elements and add them to the DOM using the `createElement()` method. After creating an element, you can append it to another element using `appendChild()`.

```javascript
let newParagraph = document.createElement("p");
newParagraph.textContent = "New sensor reading:
25°C";
document.getElementById("sensor-
readings").appendChild(newParagraph);
```

Similarly, you can remove elements from the DOM using `removeChild()`:

```javascript
let paragraphToRemove =
document.getElementById("temperature");
paragraphToRemove.parentNode.removeChild(paragraphToR
emove);
```

4. Handling Events

Events are a key part of DOM manipulation. They allow you to respond to user actions such as clicks, keystrokes, or mouse movements. You can listen for events on elements using `addEventListener()`.

```javascript
let button = document.querySelector("button");
button.addEventListener("click", function() {
```

```
    console.log("Button clicked!");
});
```

In this example, we listen for the `click` event on the button, and when it's clicked, the callback function is executed.

Project: Building a Live Dashboard

Now that we've covered the basics of DOM manipulation, let's apply what we've learned to create a live dashboard. This dashboard will simulate real-time sensor readings for a production line. The key components of the dashboard will include:

- A display area showing current sensor readings for temperature, pressure, and speed.
- A button that simulates updating the sensor readings every few seconds.

Step 1: Structuring the HTML

We'll start by setting up the basic HTML structure for our dashboard:

```
html
```

```html
<!DOCTYPE html>
<html lang="en">
```

```
<head>
    <meta charset="UTF-8">
    <meta name="viewport" content="width=device-
width, initial-scale=1.0">
    <title>Live Dashboard</title>
</head>
<body>
    <h1>Production Line Dashboard</h1>
    <div id="sensor-readings">
        <p>Temperature: <span
id="temperature">20°C</span></p>
        <p>Pressure: <span id="pressure">1013
hPa</span></p>
        <p>Speed: <span id="speed">0 rpm</span></p>
    </div>
    <button id="updateButton">Update
Readings</button>
    <script src="app.js"></script>
</body>
</html>
```

Step 2: Creating JavaScript Functions for Simulating Data

Now let's write the JavaScript to simulate updating the sensor readings. We'll create random values for each sensor every time the button is clicked.

```
javascript
```

```
document.getElementById("updateButton").addEventListe
ner("click", function() {
    let temperature = (Math.random() * 10 +
20).toFixed(1) + "°C";
    let pressure = (Math.random() * 10 +
1010).toFixed(1) + " hPa";
    let speed = (Math.random() * 10).toFixed(1) + "
rpm";
```

```
document.getElementById("temperature").textContent =
temperature;
    document.getElementById("pressure").textContent =
pressure;
    document.getElementById("speed").textContent =
speed;
});
```

In this code, we generate random values for temperature, pressure, and speed. When the button is clicked, the readings are updated with the new simulated data.

Step 3: Adding a Timer for Auto-Updates

To simulate real-time data, we can set up an interval that automatically updates the sensor readings every few seconds.

```
javascript
```

```
setInterval(function() {
    let temperature = (Math.random() * 10 +
20).toFixed(1) + "°C";
    let pressure = (Math.random() * 10 +
1010).toFixed(1) + " hPa";
    let speed = (Math.random() * 10).toFixed(1) + "
rpm";


document.getElementById("temperature").textContent =
temperature;
    document.getElementById("pressure").textContent =
pressure;
    document.getElementById("speed").textContent =
speed;
}, 3000);
```

This will update the readings every 3 seconds, simulating live data updates.

Key Takeaways

In this chapter, you've learned how to manipulate the DOM using JavaScript. You've explored how to query elements, create new elements, update their content, and remove them from the page. You've also seen how to handle events and create interactive web pages. Finally, you applied this knowledge by building a live dashboard that simulates real-time sensor readings for a production line.

Chapter 6: Responding to Users — Event Handling

In modern web development, user interaction is at the heart of any application. Without user input, websites and applications would be static and lifeless. JavaScript provides powerful tools for responding to user actions, making web pages dynamic, interactive, and engaging. Whether it's a button click, a form submission, or a custom event, JavaScript's **event handling** capabilities allow you to detect and respond to these actions in real-time.

In this chapter, we'll explore the core concepts of event handling in JavaScript, including how to **attach event listeners** for various user actions such as clicks, input, forms, and even custom events. We'll also build a practical project: an order form with **inline validation** and **success/error messages**, which will help you understand how to handle events in a real-world scenario.

By the end of this chapter, you'll have a solid understanding of how to listen for and respond to events in JavaScript, how to improve the user experience (UX) with feedback loops, and how to implement best practices like **debouncing input** and **event delegation**.

Introduction to Event Handling

An event in JavaScript is an action that occurs as a result of a user's interaction with a webpage. Examples of events include clicking a button, typing in a text field, submitting a form, or even moving the mouse. JavaScript provides a way to **listen** for these events and run specific code when they occur.

When you add an event listener to an element, you're telling the browser to **watch** for specific actions on that element. Once the action happens, the corresponding function (also known as an event handler) is executed.

In JavaScript, there are two main ways to handle events:

1. **Using event listeners**: This is the modern, recommended approach.
2. **Using HTML event attributes**: This method is older and not as flexible.

We'll focus on the more versatile and flexible event listeners approach.

Attaching Event Listeners

An **event listener** is a function that listens for a specific event and executes code in response. You attach event listeners to DOM elements using the `addEventListener()` method. This method allows you to specify the type of event you want to listen for and the function to execute when that event occurs.

Here's the syntax for `addEventListener()`:

```javascript
element.addEventListener("event", function, useCapture);
```

- **event**: The type of event you want to listen for (e.g., `click`, `input`, `submit`).
- **function**: The function to execute when the event occurs.
- **useCapture**: This is an optional boolean argument, which determines the order in which events are handled (we'll leave this for later).

Let's start with a simple example. Imagine you have a button, and you want to respond when it's clicked:

```html
html

<button id="submitButton">Submit</button>
<script>
    let button =
document.getElementById("submitButton");
    button.addEventListener("click", function() {
        alert("Button clicked!");
    });
</script>
```

In this example, the button with the ID `submitButton` listens for the `click` event. When the button is clicked, the event handler is executed, and an alert appears with the message "Button clicked!".

Event Types

JavaScript provides a wide range of events that you can listen for. Below are some of the most commonly used event types:

1. Click Events

The `click` event is triggered when a user clicks an element, such as a button, link, or image. You can attach a `click` event listener to any clickable element.

```
javascript

document.querySelector("#button").addEventListener("c
lick", function() {
    console.log("Button clicked!");
});
```

2. Input and Change Events

The `input` event is triggered when the user types into an `<input>`, `<textarea>`, or `<select>` element. This event is ideal for real-time validation or showing feedback as the user types.

```
javascript

document.querySelector("#inputField").addEventListene
r("input", function() {
    console.log("Input field changed!");
});
```

The `change` event, on the other hand, is triggered when the value of a form element changes, and the element loses focus (for `<input>`, `<select>`, or `<textarea>`).

```
javascript

document.querySelector("#dropdown").addEventListener(
"change", function() {
    console.log("Dropdown value changed!");
```

```
});
```

3. Form Submission Events

The `submit` event is fired when a form is submitted. This event is commonly used to validate the form before it's sent to the server.

```
javascript
```

```javascript
document.querySelector("#myForm").addEventListener("s
ubmit", function(event) {
    event.preventDefault(); // Prevents the form from
actually submitting
    console.log("Form submitted!");
});
```

4. Mouse and Keyboard Events

JavaScript also provides events for detecting mouse movements, clicks, and keyboard actions. These include `mousemove`, `mousedown`, `mouseup`, `keydown`, and `keyup`. These events are especially useful for interactive applications, such as drag-and-drop features or game controls.

```
javascript
```

```javascript
document.querySelector("#textInput").addEventListener
("keydown", function(event) {
    console.log("Key pressed: " + event.key);
});
```

Event Handling in Practice: Order Form with Inline Validation

To demonstrate event handling in a real-world scenario, we'll build an **order form** that allows users to enter their information. The form will feature **inline validation** to ensure the user enters valid data. If the data is valid, a success message will be displayed; otherwise, an error message will show up.

Step 1: Setting Up the HTML Structure

Let's start by creating the basic structure for the order form:

html

```
<form id="orderForm">
    <label for="name">Full Name</label>
    <input type="text" id="name" name="name"
required>
    <div id="nameError" style="color: red;"></div>

    <label for="email">Email</label>
    <input type="email" id="email" name="email"
required>
    <div id="emailError" style="color: red;"></div>
```

```
    <label for="quantity">Quantity</label>
    <input type="number" id="quantity"
name="quantity" required>
    <div id="quantityError" style="color:
red;"></div>

    <button type="submit">Place Order</button>
    <div id="formStatus"></div>
</form>
```

In this form, we have fields for **name, email,** and **quantity,** each with an error message container below them. The form will be submitted when the user clicks the "Place Order" button.

Step 2: Implementing Inline Validation

Next, we'll write JavaScript to handle the validation for each field. We'll listen for the `input` event on each field to validate the input as the user types.

javascript

```javascript
let form = document.getElementById("orderForm");

form.addEventListener("submit", function(event) {
    event.preventDefault(); // Prevent the form from
submitting automatically

    // Clear previous error messages
```

```
    document.getElementById("nameError").textContent
= "";
    document.getElementById("emailError").textContent
= "";

document.getElementById("quantityError").textContent
= "";

    let isValid = true;

    // Name Validation
    let name = document.getElementById("name").value;
    if (name.trim() === "") {

document.getElementById("nameError").textContent =
"Name is required!";
        isValid = false;
    }


    // Email Validation
    let email =
document.getElementById("email").value;
    let emailPattern = /^[^ ]+@[^ ]+\.[a-z]{2,3}$/;
    if (!emailPattern.test(email)) {

document.getElementById("emailError").textContent =
"Please enter a valid email address!";
        isValid = false;
    }
```

```
    // Quantity Validation
    let quantity =
document.getElementById("quantity").value;
    if (quantity <= 0) {

document.getElementById("quantityError").textContent
= "Quantity must be greater than 0!";
        isValid = false;
    }

    // Show success or error message based on
validation
    let statusMessage =
document.getElementById("formStatus");
    if (isValid) {
        statusMessage.textContent = "Order placed
successfully!";
        statusMessage.style.color = "green";
    } else {
        statusMessage.textContent = "Please fix the
errors above.";
        statusMessage.style.color = "red";
    }
});
```

In this script:

- We attach an event listener to the form for the `submit` event.

- The form's default behavior is prevented using `event.preventDefault()` so we can handle validation manually.
- For each input field, we check if the value is valid and display an error message if it's not.
- If all fields are valid, a success message is shown; otherwise, an error message appears.

Step 3: Adding Debouncing for Real-Time Input Validation

Debouncing is a technique used to limit the number of times an event handler is called. For input validation, this can be useful to prevent the validation function from firing every time the user types a character. Instead, the function is called only after the user stops typing for a certain period.

Here's how to add debouncing to the email field:

javascript

```
let emailInput = document.getElementById("email");
let debounceTimer;

emailInput.addEventListener("input", function() {
    clearTimeout(debounceTimer);

    debounceTimer = setTimeout(function() {
```

```
    let email = emailInput.value;
    let emailPattern = /^[^ ]+@[^ ]+\.[a-
z]{2,3}$/;
    let errorMessage =
document.getElementById("emailError");

    if (!emailPattern.test(email)) {
        errorMessage.textContent = "Please enter
a valid email address!";
    } else {
        errorMessage.textContent = "";
    }
}, 500); // Wait 500 milliseconds after the user
stops typing
});
```

This ensures that the email validation only runs after the user has stopped typing for 500 milliseconds, improving performance and user experience.

Step 4: Event Delegation for Dynamic Content

Event delegation is a technique where you attach an event listener to a parent element rather than individual child elements. This is especially useful when dealing with dynamic content or large numbers of elements.

Here's an example using event delegation to listen for clicks on a list of items:

```javascript
document.getElementById("orderForm").addEventListener
("click", function(event) {
    if (event.target &&
event.target.matches("button")) {
        console.log("Button clicked: " +
event.target.textContent);
    }
});
```

In this example, we attach a `click` event listener to the form element itself. If the click target matches a button, we handle the event. This works even if buttons are added dynamically to the form.

Key Takeaways

By the end of this chapter, you should feel confident handling user input and responding to events in JavaScript. You've learned how to:

- Attach event listeners to elements for various user interactions.

- Use input validation to ensure that data entered by users is correct.
- Implement debouncing to improve performance and reduce unnecessary event triggers.
- Use event delegation to handle events for dynamically added content.

With this foundation, you can create interactive, dynamic applications that provide real-time feedback to users

Chapter 7: Talking to Servers — Fetch and AJAX

In modern web development, a significant portion of creating dynamic applications involves fetching and sending data to and from a server. Whether you're pulling data to display on a dashboard, submitting a form, or interacting with a third-party API, understanding how to communicate with servers is essential. Two common methods used in JavaScript for handling HTTP requests are **Fetch API** and **AJAX (Asynchronous JavaScript and XML)**. In this chapter, we will focus on using **Fetch** to request and send data, handling responses, and managing errors effectively.

We'll explore how to interact with web APIs, particularly focusing on fetching JSON data, working with headers, handling query parameters, and addressing common error states. The project at hand will simulate pulling live weather data for an **automated irrigation system dashboard**, allowing users to get weather updates and adjust irrigation settings based on real-time conditions.

By the end of this chapter, you'll be well-equipped to make HTTP requests, manage responses, and ensure smooth, user-friendly interactions with remote servers.

Understanding Fetch and AJAX

Before we dive into specifics, let's first understand the difference between **Fetch API** and **AJAX**, and why **Fetch** is the modern choice for handling HTTP requests in JavaScript.

1. AJAX

AJAX stands for **Asynchronous JavaScript and XML**, a technique used to send and receive data asynchronously from the server without refreshing the page. AJAX has been widely used since the early 2000s and is fundamental to creating dynamic web applications. The XMLHttpRequest object was the primary way of handling AJAX requests before newer technologies like Fetch came into play.

Here's an example of a simple AJAX request:

```javascript
let xhr = new XMLHttpRequest();
xhr.open("GET", "https://api.example.com/data",
true);
xhr.onreadystatechange = function () {
    if (xhr.readyState == 4 && xhr.status == 200) {
        let data = JSON.parse(xhr.responseText);
```

```
        console.log(data);
    }
};
xhr.send();
```

While AJAX works fine, it's relatively verbose, especially when it comes to handling complex requests like sending JSON or dealing with promises.

2. Fetch API

The **Fetch API** is the modern way to make HTTP requests in JavaScript. It's cleaner, more flexible, and easier to work with compared to XMLHttpRequest. Fetch returns a **Promise**, which is a more powerful abstraction for handling asynchronous operations.

Here's how you might make the same request using Fetch:

javascript

```
fetch("https://api.example.com/data")
    .then(response => response.json())
    .then(data => console.log(data))
    .catch(error => console.error('Error:', error));
```

The Fetch API makes it much easier to handle requests and responses, and it's widely supported by all modern browsers.

Making a Basic Fetch Request

Now, let's dive into the specifics of making fetch requests in JavaScript. The `fetch()` method allows you to make network requests to retrieve or send data. Here's a basic example of how to use it:

```javascript
fetch("https://api.example.com/data")
    .then(response => response.json()) // Convert
response to JSON
    .then(data => console.log(data))     // Log the
response data
    .catch(error => console.error(error)); // Handle
any errors
```

This is a basic GET request. When you use `fetch()`, it returns a promise that resolves to the `Response` object, which represents the response to the request. You can then call methods like `.json()` to parse the response body into JSON.

Handling Headers

When making requests, you might need to send custom headers or handle headers in the response. Headers contain metadata about the request or response, like authentication tokens or content type.

Here's how to handle headers with Fetch:

```javascript
fetch("https://api.example.com/data", {
    method: "GET",
    headers: {
        "Content-Type": "application/json",
        "Authorization": "Bearer your_token_here"
    }
})
    .then(response => response.json())
    .then(data => console.log(data))
    .catch(error => console.error('Error:', error));
```

In this example:

- We're specifying the method (`GET`).
- We're adding custom headers, including `Content-Type` and `Authorization`.

Handling Response Status and Error States

One of the most important parts of working with fetch is handling errors and checking the response status. While fetch won't reject an HTTP error (like a 404 or 500), it's important to manually check for these types of errors and handle them appropriately.

Here's how you might check the response status:

```javascript
fetch("https://api.example.com/data")
    .then(response => {
        if (!response.ok) {
            throw new Error(`HTTP error! Status:
${response.status}`);
        }
        return response.json();
    })
    .then(data => console.log(data))
    .catch(error => console.error('Error:', error));
```

In this example:

- `response.ok` is a boolean that indicates if the response was successful (status code 200-299).
- If the response is not okay, an error is thrown, and it's caught in the `catch()` block.

Working with JSON Data

Most APIs return data in the **JSON** format, which is easy to work with in JavaScript. The .json() method on the Response object is used to parse the response body into a JavaScript object.

Here's an example of fetching data and parsing it as JSON:

javascript

```
fetch("https://api.example.com/weather")
    .then(response => response.json())
    .then(data => {
        console.log(data.temperature); // Example:
output temperature
    })
    .catch(error => console.error("Error fetching
data:", error));
```

In this example, data is a JavaScript object containing the parsed JSON from the API. You can then easily access its properties like data.temperature.

Working with Query Parameters

Many times, you'll need to pass **query parameters** to an API to filter or refine the data you're requesting. Query parameters are added to the URL after a ? and are typically formatted like key=value.

Let's say we want to fetch weather data for a specific city. Here's how you can add query parameters to the URL:

javascript

```javascript
let city = "New York";
let apiKey = "your_api_key";

fetch(`https://api.weather.com/data?city=${city}&apik
ey=${apiKey}`)
    .then(response => response.json())
    .then(data => console.log(data))
    .catch(error => console.error('Error:', error));
```

In this example, we've dynamically added the city and API key as query parameters to the URL. This is a common pattern for making API calls.

Project: Pulling Live Weather Data for an Automated Irrigation System

In this section, we'll build an **automated irrigation system dashboard** that pulls live weather data from an API and adjusts irrigation settings accordingly. The system will fetch weather data, display it on the dashboard, and calculate irrigation needs based on weather conditions such as temperature, humidity, and rainfall.

Step 1: Set Up the HTML Structure

Let's start by setting up the HTML for the dashboard. We'll display the current temperature, humidity, and rainfall, and a button to fetch new data.

html

```
<!DOCTYPE html>
<html lang="en">
<head>
    <meta charset="UTF-8">
    <meta name="viewport" content="width=device-
width, initial-scale=1.0">
    <title>Irrigation System Dashboard</title>
</head>
<body>
    <h1>Automated Irrigation System</h1>
    <div>
```

```
        <p>Temperature: <span
id="temperature">Loading...</span></p>
        <p>Humidity: <span
id="humidity">Loading...</span></p>
        <p>Rainfall: <span
id="rainfall">Loading...</span></p>
        <button id="refreshButton">Refresh Weather
Data</button>
    </div>
    <script src="app.js"></script>
</body>
</html>
```

Step 2: Fetching Weather Data

Now, let's write the JavaScript to fetch weather data from an API. We'll use a placeholder API (for example, OpenWeatherMap) that provides real-time weather information.

javascript

```javascript
document.getElementById("refreshButton").addEventList
ener("click", function() {
    let apiKey = "your_api_key";
    let city = "New York";


fetch(`https://api.openweathermap.org/data/2.5/weathe
r?q=${city}&appid=${apiKey}`)
        .then(response => response.json())
```

```
        .then(data => {
            let temperature = data.main.temp;
            let humidity = data.main.humidity;
            let rainfall = data.weather[0].main ===
"Rain" ? "Yes" : "No";


document.getElementById("temperature").textContent =
`${temperature}°C`;

document.getElementById("humidity").textContent =
`${humidity}%`;

document.getElementById("rainfall").textContent =
rainfall;
        })
        .catch(error => {
            console.error('Error:', error);
            alert("There was an error fetching
weather data.");
        });
});
```

In this example:

- We use the OpenWeatherMap API to get the current weather for a specific city.
- We display the temperature, humidity, and whether there's rain.

- The button allows the user to refresh the data.

Step 3: Adjusting Irrigation Based on Weather

Now let's extend the functionality by adding logic to adjust the irrigation system based on the weather conditions. For example, if it's raining, we don't need to irrigate the fields. If it's very hot and dry, we might need more water.

javascript

```javascript
function adjustIrrigation(temperature, humidity,
rainfall) {
    let irrigationStatus = "";

    if (rainfall === "Yes") {
        irrigationStatus = "No need for irrigation,
it's raining!";
    } else if (temperature > 30 && humidity < 50) {
        irrigationStatus = "High temperature and low
humidity. Increase irrigation!";
    } else if (temperature < 10) {
        irrigationStatus = "Temperature is too low.
No irrigation needed.";
    } else {
        irrigationStatus = "Normal conditions.
Regular irrigation.";
    }
```

```
        console.log(irrigationStatus); // Display in
console or UI
}
```

We'll call `adjustIrrigation()` after fetching the weather data:

javascript

```
.then(data => {
    let temperature = data.main.temp;
    let humidity = data.main.humidity;
    let rainfall = data.weather[0].main === "Rain" ?
"Yes" : "No";



document.getElementById("temperature").textContent =
`${temperature}°C`;
    document.getElementById("humidity").textContent =
`${humidity}%`;
    document.getElementById("rainfall").textContent =
rainfall;


    adjustIrrigation(temperature, humidity,
rainfall); // Adjust irrigation based on weather
})
```

Key Takeaways

In this chapter, you've learned how to:

- Use the Fetch API to request data from a server and handle the response.
- Work with JSON data and parse it into JavaScript objects.
- Add query parameters to your requests to filter or refine the data.
- Handle errors in fetch requests, including managing failed or slow requests.
- Build a real-world application, like a live weather dashboard for an irrigation system.

Asynchronous data fetching is a crucial part of creating dynamic, real-time applications. Mastering **Fetch** and understanding **CORS** (Cross-Origin Resource Sharing) and **REST** principles will allow you to create powerful applications that can interact with external services and provide users with real-time data.

Chapter 8: Handling Asynchronous Workflows

In JavaScript, asynchronous programming is the key to building efficient, user-friendly applications. It's essential for any web application that needs to perform tasks like fetching data from a server, reading files, or performing calculations without freezing the user interface. Without understanding how to manage asynchronous workflows, your app can become slow, unresponsive, and hard to maintain.

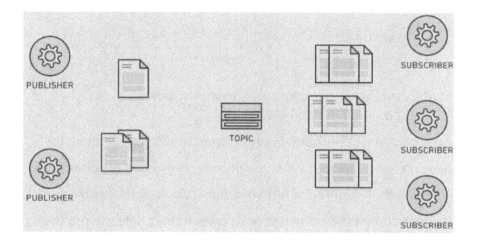

In this chapter, we will dive deep into **Promises**, the `.then()` and `.catch()` methods, and **async/await** syntax—tools that help you handle asynchronous operations in JavaScript. We'll also explore how to simulate fetching patient records in a healthcare app, implementing loading states to improve user experience. This will give you practical experience in managing asynchronous data flow, and allow you to apply best practices like chaining operations and handling errors gracefully.

By the end of this chapter, you will understand how asynchronous programming works, how to use Promises to handle multiple tasks, and how to cleanly structure your code to avoid common pitfalls like **callback hell**. You'll also gain insight into advanced techniques, including chaining multiple Promises, using async functions, and handling errors in a way that keeps your application running smoothly.

Understanding Asynchronous Programming

At its core, **asynchronous programming** allows your program to perform multiple tasks at once. Unlike **synchronous programming**, where each task runs one after the other (blocking the program until the task completes), asynchronous programming lets you run tasks in the background while your program continues executing other instructions. This is especially useful for web applications that rely heavily on fetching data, interacting with APIs, or processing user input without causing the page to reload or freeze.

JavaScript uses an event-driven, non-blocking model, meaning that operations that might take time (like fetching data from an API or reading a file) won't block the execution of the rest of the code. This makes JavaScript perfect for building dynamic, fast, and interactive applications.

To manage this non-blocking behavior, JavaScript has several techniques for handling asynchronous code:

1. **Callbacks**: Functions passed as arguments to other functions.
2. **Promises**: Objects that represent the eventual completion (or failure) of an asynchronous operation.
3. **Async/Await**: Syntax that allows for more readable and synchronous-like handling of asynchronous code.

In this chapter, we'll focus on **Promises** and **async/await**, as these are the modern and preferred methods for handling asynchronous workflows in JavaScript.

Promises: The Foundation of Asynchronous Workflows

A **Promise** is an object that represents the eventual completion or failure of an asynchronous operation. A Promise can be in one of three states:

1. **Pending**: The operation is still in progress.
2. **Fulfilled**: The operation completed successfully.
3. **Rejected**: The operation failed, usually due to an error.

A Promise allows you to handle asynchronous operations in a more predictable and manageable way compared to callbacks. Let's take a look at how to create a Promise and use it.

Creating a Promise

A Promise is created using the `new Promise()` constructor. The constructor takes a function as an argument, called the **executor function**, which has two parameters: `resolve` and `reject`.

- `resolve` is called when the asynchronous operation completes successfully.
- `reject` is called if the operation fails.

Here's an example of a Promise that simulates a successful operation after a delay:

javascript

```
let fetchData = new Promise((resolve, reject) => {
    setTimeout(() => {
        let success = true; // Simulate success or
failure
        if (success) {
```

```
        resolve("Data fetched successfully!");
    } else {
        reject("Error: Failed to fetch data.");
    }
  }, 2000); // Simulate a delay of 2 seconds
});
```

In this example:

- After 2 seconds, the Promise either resolves or rejects based on the value of the `success` variable.
- `resolve()` is called if the operation is successful, and `reject()` is called if there's an error.

Handling Promises with `.then()` *and* `.catch()`

Once a Promise is created, we can **handle** its result using `.then()` and `.catch()`.

- `.then()` is called when the Promise is fulfilled (i.e., the asynchronous operation is successful).
- `.catch()` is used to handle errors when the Promise is rejected.

Here's how you handle the successful and failed cases:

```javascript
```

```
fetchData
    .then((result) => {
        console.log(result); // Output: Data fetched
successfully!
    })
    .catch((error) => {
        console.error(error); // Output: Error:
Failed to fetch data.
    });
```

The `.then()` method takes a callback function that will be executed if the Promise resolves. Similarly, `.catch()` handles any errors that occur.

Chaining Promises

One of the biggest advantages of using Promises is the ability to **chain** multiple asynchronous operations. Each `.then()` method returns a new Promise, which allows you to chain additional actions.

```javascript
fetchData
    .then((result) => {
        console.log(result); // First success
        return new Promise((resolve) => resolve("Next
step complete"));
    })
    .then((result) => {
```

```
        console.log(result); // Second success
    })
    .catch((error) => {
        console.error(error); // Handle any errors
    });
```

This pattern is especially useful when you need to perform several asynchronous actions in a sequence, such as fetching data from multiple sources or performing complex calculations.

Handling Errors in Promises

Error handling is crucial when working with asynchronous code. Without proper error handling, a failed Promise could leave your application in an unknown state, leading to unexpected behavior. Thankfully, Promises provide a robust mechanism for handling errors using .catch().

Here's an example where we simulate a failed network request:

javascript

```javascript
let fetchData = new Promise((resolve, reject) => {
    setTimeout(() => {
        let success = false; // Simulate failure
        if (success) {
            resolve("Data fetched successfully!");
```

```
    } else {
        reject("Error: Failed to fetch data.");
    }
}, 2000);
});

fetchData
    .then((result) => {
        console.log(result);
    })
    .catch((error) => {
        console.error(error); // Output: Error:
Failed to fetch data.
    });
```

In this case, the `.catch()` block will capture the rejection, preventing the application from crashing and ensuring that you can handle the error gracefully.

Async/Await: Making Asynchronous Code Look Synchronous

While Promises provide a more readable alternative to traditional callback-based asynchronous programming, they can still lead to somewhat cluttered code when dealing with multiple operations. The **async/await** syntax allows you to write asynchronous code in a synchronous-like manner, making it even easier to read and maintain.

1. Async Functions

An **async function** is a function that always returns a **Promise**. Inside an async function, you can use the `await` keyword to pause execution until a Promise is resolved or rejected.

Here's an example of an async function that fetches data:

javascript

```javascript
async function fetchData() {
    return "Data fetched successfully!";
}

fetchData().then(result => console.log(result)); //
Output: Data fetched successfully!
```

The `fetchData()` function is asynchronous and returns a Promise. By default, async functions always return a Promise, which makes them easy to integrate with other asynchronous workflows.

2. Using `await`

The `await` keyword is used inside an async function to pause execution until a Promise resolves. It makes asynchronous code look like synchronous code, simplifying complex workflows.

Here's an example of using `await` to wait for a Promise to resolve:

javascript

```javascript
async function fetchWeatherData() {
    let response = await
fetch("https://api.openweathermap.org/data/2.5/weathe
r?q=New York&appid=your_api_key");
    let data = await response.json();
    return data;
}

fetchWeatherData().then(data => console.log(data));
```

In this example:

- The `await` keyword pauses the execution of `fetchWeatherData()` until the `fetch()` Promise resolves.
- The `await` keyword can only be used inside `async` functions.

3. Error Handling with Async/Await

Error handling is a critical part of working with async/await. To catch errors in an async function, we use **try/catch** blocks, just like synchronous code.

Here's how to handle errors when using async/await:

```javascript
async function fetchWeatherData() {
    try {
        let response = await
fetch("https://api.openweathermap.org/data/2.5/weathe
r?q=New York&appid=your_api_key");
        let data = await response.json();
        return data;
    } catch (error) {
        console.error("Error fetching weather data:",
error);
    }
}

fetchWeatherData();
```

In this example:

- The `try` block contains the code that might throw an error
  (e.g., the fetch request).

- The `catch` block handles any errors that occur and logs the error message.

Project: Simulating Fetching Patient Records

Let's apply these concepts in a **healthcare app** where we simulate fetching patient records. In this app, we'll display a loading state while data is being fetched, and update the user interface once the data is retrieved.

Step 1: Simulating Data Fetching

For the sake of this project, we'll simulate an API that returns patient data. Here's how we can simulate fetching patient records using a Promise:

javascript

```javascript
function fetchPatientRecords() {
    return new Promise((resolve, reject) => {
        setTimeout(() => {
            let success = true; // Simulate a
successful response
            if (success) {
                resolve({
                    name: "John Doe",
```

```
                age: 45,
                diagnosis: "Hypertension"
            });
        } else {
            reject("Failed to fetch patient
records.");
        }
    }, 2000); // Simulate 2 seconds delay
  });
}
```

In this code:

- `fetchPatientRecords()` simulates a network request that either resolves with patient data or rejects with an error message after 2 seconds.

Step 2: Displaying a Loading State

Now, let's create a basic UI with a loading indicator while the patient data is being fetched.

html

```html
<div id="patientInfo">
    <h1>Patient Records</h1>
    <p id="loadingMessage">Loading patient
data...</p>
    <p id="patientDetails"></p>
```

```
</div>
```

We'll update the `loadingMessage` while the data is being fetched and display the patient details once the data is retrieved.

```javascript
async function displayPatientInfo() {

document.getElementById("loadingMessage").textContent
= "Loading patient data...";

    try {
        let patientData = await
fetchPatientRecords();

document.getElementById("loadingMessage").style.displ
ay = "none";

document.getElementById("patientDetails").textContent
= `Name: ${patientData.name}, Age:
${patientData.age}, Diagnosis:
${patientData.diagnosis}`;
    } catch (error) {

document.getElementById("loadingMessage").style.color
= "red";
```

```
document.getElementById("loadingMessage").textContent
= `Error: ${error}`;
    }
}
```

```
displayPatientInfo();
```

In this example:

- While the patient data is being fetched, the "Loading patient data..." message is displayed.
- Once the data is retrieved, the loading message is hidden and the patient details are shown.
- If there's an error, the loading message turns red and displays an error message.

Key Takeaways

By the end of this chapter, you should now be comfortable with:

- Using **Promises** to handle asynchronous operations and manage workflows.
- Handling success and failure scenarios with `.then()` and `.catch()`.

- Using **async/await** to write more readable asynchronous code.
- Managing error handling and implementing robust workflows for fetching data.
- Implementing a real-world example by simulating patient record fetching in a healthcare app, including using loading states to enhance the user experience.

With these skills, you are now equipped to handle complex asynchronous operations, making your applications responsive, reliable, and easy to maintain.

Chapter 9: Modern JS Essentials (ES6+)

JavaScript is a constantly evolving language, and staying up to date with the latest features is key to writing clean, efficient, and maintainable code. The **ES6+** (ECMAScript 2015 and beyond) updates introduced several powerful new features that have revolutionized the way developers write JavaScript. These features improve code readability, reduce redundancy, and make JavaScript easier to work with, especially in complex applications.

In this chapter, we will dive deep into some of the most essential modern JavaScript features: `let`/`const`, **template literals**, **destructuring**, **spread/rest operators**, **classes**, and **modules**. These features are integral to writing modern, modular JavaScript, and they will form the foundation for more complex codebases.

Our project for this chapter will involve creating a small **logistics helper library** and packaging it as an **ES module**. By the end of this chapter, you will have not only mastered these modern JavaScript concepts but also learned how to modularize your code for greater reuse and scalability.

Let and Const: Block-Scoped Variables

Before ES6, JavaScript only had the `var` keyword for declaring variables. While `var` works, it has some quirks that can cause issues, especially when dealing with scope and block-level scoping. ES6 introduced two new ways to declare variables: `let` and `const`. These two keywords provide **block-scoping** and address many of the problems that developers commonly face with `var`.

1. `let`: Block-scoped Variables

The `let` keyword allows you to declare a variable that is scoped to the nearest enclosing block (i.e., within { }), rather than the function or global scope. This gives you more predictable and less error-prone behavior when dealing with variable scopes.

Example:

javascript

```
if (true) {
    let x = 10;
    console.log(x); // 10
}
console.log(x); // ReferenceError: x is not defined
```

In this example, `x` is only available inside the `if` block because it was declared with `let`. This prevents you from accidentally accessing variables outside their intended scope.

2. `const`: *Block-scoped Constants*

The `const` keyword is used to declare constants—variables that should not be reassigned after their initial assignment. Like `let`, `const` is block-scoped, but it has an important difference: once a value is assigned to a `const` variable, it cannot be reassigned.

Example:

```javascript
const pi = 3.14159;
pi = 3.14; // TypeError: Assignment to constant
variable.
```

`const` is especially useful for values that should never change, such as mathematical constants or configuration values.

Template Literals: Simplifying String Concatenation

One of the most tedious tasks in JavaScript before ES6 was **string concatenation**. For example, if you wanted to combine a string with a variable, you had to use the + operator:

```
javascript
```

```
let name = "John";
let greeting = "Hello, " + name + "!";
```

While this works, it's cumbersome and can become hard to read when you're dealing with complex strings or variables. ES6 introduced **template literals**, which allow for easier string interpolation and multi-line strings using backticks (`` ` ``).

1. String Interpolation

Template literals allow you to embed variables directly within a string using ${ }. This makes the code cleaner and more readable:

```
javascript
```

```
let name = "John";
let greeting = `Hello, ${name}!`;
console.log(greeting); // Output: Hello, John!
```

You can even perform expressions inside ${ }:

```
javascript
```

```
let a = 5;
let b = 3;
let sum = `The sum of ${a} and ${b} is ${a + b}`;
console.log(sum); // Output: The sum of 5 and 3 is 8
```

2. Multi-line Strings

Template literals also allow for multi-line strings, which eliminates the need for cumbersome concatenation or escape characters for new lines:

```javascript
let message = `This is a string
that spans multiple
lines.`;
console.log(message);
```

This feature makes template literals highly useful for generating content, especially in dynamic web applications.

Destructuring: Extracting Values from Arrays and Objects

Destructuring is a powerful feature that simplifies extracting values from arrays and objects, making the code cleaner and reducing the need for repetitive variable assignments.

1. Array Destructuring

With array destructuring, you can assign individual elements of an array to variables without needing to access each element by index:

```
javascript
```

```javascript
let numbers = [1, 2, 3, 4];
let [first, second, third] = numbers;
console.log(first, second, third); // Output: 1 2 3
```

This approach is much cleaner than manually extracting values:

```
javascript
```

```javascript
let first = numbers[0];
let second = numbers[1];
let third = numbers[2];
```

2. Object Destructuring

Object destructuring works in a similar way, allowing you to assign properties of an object to variables with matching names:

```
javascript
```

```javascript
let person = { name: "Alice", age: 30 };
let { name, age } = person;
console.log(name, age); // Output: Alice 30
```

You can also rename variables using the : syntax:

```
javascript
```

```javascript
let { name: fullName, age: yearsOld } = person;
```

```
console.log(fullName, yearsOld); // Output: Alice 30
```

3. Nested Destructuring

Destructuring can be used with nested objects and arrays as well, making it even more powerful when dealing with complex data structures:

```javascript
let user = {
    id: 1,
    profile: {
        name: "Alice",
        age: 30
    }
};

let { profile: { name, age } } = user;
console.log(name, age); // Output: Alice 30
```

Spread and Rest Operators: Expanding and Collecting Data

ES6 introduced two very useful operators: the **spread operator** (...) and the **rest operator** (...). Though they share the same syntax, they serve different purposes depending on the context.

1. Spread Operator

The **spread operator** allows you to "spread" the elements of an array or the properties of an object into another array or object. It's particularly useful for ing or combining arrays and objects.

- **For Arrays**:

javascript

```
let arr1 = [1, 2, 3];
let arr2 = [...arr1, 4, 5]; // ing arr1 and adding
new elements
console.log(arr2); // Output: [1, 2, 3, 4, 5]
```

- **For Objects**:

javascript

```
let obj1 = { name: "Alice", age: 30 };
let obj2 = { ...obj1, city: "New York" }; // ing obj1
and adding a new property
console.log(obj2); // Output: { name: "Alice", age:
30, city: "New York" }
```

The spread operator is especially useful for working with immutable data structures or merging multiple objects or arrays.

2. Rest Operator

The **rest operator** allows you to collect multiple elements into an array. This is particularly useful for handling function arguments or collecting properties from an object.

- **For Functions**:

javascript

```javascript
function sum(...numbers) {
    return numbers.reduce((acc, curr) => acc + curr,
0);
}
console.log(sum(1, 2, 3, 4)); // Output: 10
```

Here, ...numbers collects all arguments passed to the function into a single array.

- **For Objects**:

javascript

```javascript
let person = { name: "Alice", age: 30, city: "New
York" };
let { name, ...rest } = person;
console.log(name); // Output: Alice
console.log(rest); // Output: { age: 30, city: "New
York" }
```

The rest operator allows you to grab all remaining properties of an object into a new object.

Classes: Object-Oriented JavaScript

Before ES6, JavaScript didn't have built-in support for creating classes in the same way other programming languages like Java or Python did. While JavaScript was always object-oriented through **prototypes,** the syntax could be clunky and hard to work with. ES6 introduced the `class` syntax, making object-oriented programming in JavaScript cleaner and more intuitive.

1. Defining Classes

In ES6, you define a class using the `class` keyword. A class can have a constructor method for initializing properties and methods to define behavior.

javascript

```javascript
class Person {
    constructor(name, age) {
        this.name = name;
        this.age = age;
    }
}
```

```
    greet() {
        console.log(`Hello, my name is ${this.name}
and I am ${this.age} years old.`);
    }
}
```

```
let person1 = new Person("Alice", 30);
person1.greet(); // Output: Hello, my name is Alice
and I am 30 years old.
```

2. Inheritance and Super

JavaScript classes support inheritance through the `extends` keyword. This allows one class to inherit properties and methods from another class.

javascript

```
class Employee extends Person {
    constructor(name, age, jobTitle) {
        super(name, age); // Call the parent class
constructor
        this.jobTitle = jobTitle;
    }

    work() {
        console.log(`${this.name} is working as a
${this.jobTitle}.`);
    }
}
```

```javascript
let employee1 = new Employee("Bob", 35, "Engineer");
employee1.greet(); // Output: Hello, my name is Bob
and I am 35 years old.
employee1.work();  // Output: Bob is working as a
Engineer.
```

3. Getters and Setters

Classes also support **getters** and **setters**, which allow you to define how a property is accessed or modified.

javascript

```javascript
class Circle {
    constructor(radius) {
        this._radius = radius;
    }

    get area() {
        return Math.PI * this._radius ** 2;
    }

    set radius(newRadius) {
        if (newRadius > 0) {
            this._radius = newRadius;
        } else {
            console.log("Radius must be positive.");
        }
    }
}
```

```
}
```

```
let circle = new Circle(5);
console.log(circle.area); // Output:
78.53981633974483
circle.radius = 10;       // Update radius
console.log(circle.area); // Output:
314.1592653589793
```

Modules: Organizing Code into Reusable Components

One of the most significant improvements with ES6 was the introduction of **modules**. Before ES6, JavaScript didn't have a standardized way to divide code into reusable components. With modules, you can import and export code between different files, making it easier to manage large projects.

1. Exporting Code

In ES6, you can export variables, functions, classes, and objects from a file so that they can be used in other files.

```javascript
// file1.js
export const name = "Alice";
export function greet() {
    console.log("Hello!");
```

```
}
```

2. Importing Code

Once you've exported code from a module, you can **import** it into another file:

javascript

```
// file2.js
import { name, greet } from './file1.js';

console.log(name); // Output: Alice
greet();           // Output: Hello!
```

3. Default Exports

You can also export a single item as the default export, which simplifies the import process:

javascript

```
// file1.js
export default function greet() {
    console.log("Hello!");
}
```

javascript

```
// file2.js
import greet from './file1.js';
```

```
greet();  // Output: Hello!
```

Project: Assembling a Small Logistics Helper Library

Let's put everything together by building a small **logistics helper library**. We'll create functions for calculating shipping costs, managing inventory, and handling orders. This library will be structured as an **ES module** so that it can be reused across different parts of an application.

Step 1: Structuring the Library

First, create a `logistics.js` file where we'll define our helper functions.

javascript

```javascript
// logistics.js
export function calculateShippingCost(weight,
distance) {
    const baseCost = 5; // cost per kilogram
    const distanceCost = 0.1 * distance; // cost per
kilometer
    return baseCost * weight + distanceCost;
}

export function trackPackage(packageId) {
```

```
    console.log(`Tracking package with ID:
${packageId}`);
}


export function inventoryUpdate(item, quantity) {
    console.log(`Updating inventory: ${item} -
${quantity} units`);
}
```

Step 2: Importing and Using the Module

Now, let's import and use these functions in another file:

```javascript
// app.js
import { calculateShippingCost, trackPackage,
inventoryUpdate } from './logistics.js';

let shippingCost = calculateShippingCost(10, 200);
console.log(`Shipping cost: $${shippingCost}`);

trackPackage("12345");

inventoryUpdate("Widget", 50);
```

By using ES modules, we've organized our code into smaller, reusable components that are easy to maintain and extend.

Key Takeaways

By the end of this chapter, you've learned:

1. How to use **let** and **const** for block-scoped variables.
2. How **template literals** simplify string handling with embedded expressions and multi-line strings.
3. How to use **destructuring** to easily extract data from arrays and objects.
4. The power of the **spread/rest operators** for simplifying data manipulation and function arguments.
5. How **classes** in ES6 enable object-oriented programming with inheritance, methods, and properties.
6. The basics of **ES modules** for structuring your JavaScript code into reusable components.
7. How to assemble a logistics helper library using modern JavaScript features.

With these skills, you are now ready to tackle more complex JavaScript applications, using modern, efficient, and maintainable code.

Chapter 10: Crafting a Single-Page Application

Building modern web applications requires creating rich, dynamic, and interactive experiences for users. A **Single-Page Application (SPA)** is a web app or website that interacts with the user by dynamically rewriting the current page, rather than loading entire new pages from the server. This approach improves the performance of the app by avoiding unnecessary page reloads and allows for a smoother, faster user experience.

In this chapter, we'll explore the fundamentals of building a Single-Page Application using client-side routing, state management, and templating. We'll walk through how to set up a simple SPA, specifically a **to-do or project tracker app**, and how to implement hashed routing, which allows users to navigate between different sections of the app (like `#/tasks` or `#/settings`) without triggering page reloads.

By the end of this chapter, you'll have a good grasp on how to manage dynamic views, maintain application state, and implement routing in a clean, efficient way. You'll also learn best practices for keeping your app lightweight and responsive, while ensuring a great user experience.

What is a Single-Page Application?

A **Single-Page Application (SPA)** is a type of web application or website that loads a single HTML page and dynamically updates it as the user interacts with the app. Unlike traditional web applications where each action (like clicking a link or submitting a form) triggers a page reload, SPAs load only the necessary data and update the view without reloading the entire page.

SPAs rely heavily on **client-side JavaScript**, which allows the web page to fetch data asynchronously and update the page content without reloading. This creates the feel of a desktop application in a web browser, providing a seamless user experience.

Advantages of SPAs:

- **Faster load times**: Once the initial page is loaded, SPAs only request small chunks of data, avoiding full page reloads.
- **Smoother user experience**: Since SPAs don't reload the page, interactions feel more like desktop applications, reducing the disruption of waiting for pages to load.
- **Reduced server load**: SPAs offload much of the work to the client, reducing the number of requests to the server and improving performance.

Challenges of SPAs:

- **SEO (Search Engine Optimization)**: Since SPAs load content dynamically, traditional search engines may have difficulty crawling and indexing content.
- **JavaScript-heavy**: SPAs rely heavily on JavaScript, which means they may not work properly in browsers with disabled JavaScript or low-performance devices.
- **State management**: Managing the state of a SPA can be tricky, especially as the app grows in complexity. You need a way to ensure the app's state is consistent and doesn't break when navigating between views.

Client-Side Routing: Navigating Within the SPA

In a traditional multi-page web application, when a user clicks a link, the browser makes a request to the server, which returns a new HTML page. In SPAs, we simulate this behavior by using **client-side routing**. This means that we update the URL and change the content of the page without actually reloading it. The browser's **History API** and **hash-based routing** allow us to manage these updates efficiently.

1. Hash-based Routing

In hash-based routing, the URL of the page includes a **hash (#)** that indicates the current view or state. For example, `#tasks` might represent the view where tasks are displayed, and `#settings` might represent the settings page. This is a simple method of implementing routing in a SPA.

Here's an example of how you might structure the URLs for a to-do application:

- `#/tasks`: The user is viewing the list of tasks.
- `#/settings`: The user is in the settings section where they can modify preferences.

When the hash changes, JavaScript listens for the change and dynamically updates the page content accordingly.

2. Implementing Hash-based Routing

We can implement hash-based routing by listening to the `hashchange` event on the `window` object. Every time the URL's hash changes, the event fires, allowing us to update the content based on the new hash.

Here's an example:

```javascript
javascript

// Simple routing function to handle hash changes
function router() {
    let hash = window.location.hash;  // Get the
current hash
    if (hash === "#/tasks") {
        showTasks();
    } else if (hash === "#/settings") {
        showSettings();
    } else {
        showHome();
    }
}


// Show tasks view
function showTasks() {
    document.getElementById("content").innerHTML =
"<h2>Tasks</h2><ul><li>Task 1</li><li>Task
2</li></ul>";
}

// Show settings view
function showSettings() {
    document.getElementById("content").innerHTML =
"<h2>Settings</h2><p>Adjust your preferences
here.</p>";
}
```

```
// Show home view (default)
function showHome() {
    document.getElementById("content").innerHTML =
"<h2>Welcome to the To-Do App</h2><p>Click on the
links to navigate.</p>";
}


// Listen for hash changes
window.addEventListener("hashchange", router);

// Initialize the router
router();
```

In this example, the `router()` function checks the current hash and displays the appropriate content based on the URL. The `hashchange` event ensures that the page content updates when the user clicks on a link or manually changes the hash in the address bar.

State Management: Keeping Track of Your Data

In SPAs, one of the biggest challenges is managing **state**. State refers to the data that your application is working with at any given time. For example, in our to-do app, the state could include the list of tasks, the current view (tasks, settings, etc.), and any user input.

1. Storing State in Memory

To keep track of state in a SPA, we typically store it in **variables or objects** in JavaScript. For small applications, you can simply use variables to store the state, but for larger applications, a more structured approach is often required, such as using **state management libraries** like Redux or Vuex.

For example, in our to-do app, we could maintain an array of tasks and update it whenever the user adds, removes, or modifies a task.

```javascript
let tasks = ["Task 1", "Task 2", "Task 3"];

function addTask(task) {
    tasks.push(task);
    updateTaskList();
}

function removeTask(index) {
    tasks.splice(index, 1);
    updateTaskList();
}

function updateTaskList() {
    document.getElementById("taskList").innerHTML =
tasks.map(task => `<li>${task}</li>`).join('');
```

```
}
```

```
// Initial rendering of tasks
updateTaskList();
```

In this example, the `tasks` array holds the current state of the to-do list. Every time a task is added or removed, the `updateTaskList()` function is called to update the DOM.

2. Managing State with Local Storage

For persistence across page reloads, you can store your application state in the **localStorage** API. This allows you to save data in the browser's local storage, so it persists even when the user refreshes or closes the browser.

Here's how you might save and load the task list from local storage:

```javascript
javascript

// Save tasks to localStorage
function saveTasks() {
    localStorage.setItem("tasks",
JSON.stringify(tasks));
}

// Load tasks from localStorage
function loadTasks() {
```

```
    let savedTasks = localStorage.getItem("tasks");
    if (savedTasks) {
        tasks = JSON.parse(savedTasks);
    }
    updateTaskList();
}


// Call loadTasks on startup
loadTasks();
```

In this case, `localStorage.setItem()` saves the tasks array to localStorage as a JSON string, and `localStorage.getItem()` retrieves the saved tasks on page load. This ensures that even if the page is reloaded, the tasks persist.

Templating: Dynamically Rendering Content

In a Single-Page Application, most of the content will be dynamically rendered. **Templating** is the process of creating HTML dynamically, based on data. You can use JavaScript to generate HTML on the fly and inject it into the DOM.

1. Manual Templating

In smaller applications, you can manually generate HTML using JavaScript. For example, in our to-do app, we can create an unordered list of tasks:

javascript

```
function renderTasks() {
    let taskListHtml = tasks.map(task => {
        return `<li>${task} <button
onclick="removeTask('${task}')">Remove</button></li>`
;
    }).join('');
    document.getElementById("taskList").innerHTML =
taskListHtml;
}
```

In this code, `tasks.map()` generates an HTML string for each task, and `join('')` combines them into a single string. This string is then inserted into the DOM using `innerHTML`.

2. Using Templating Engines

For larger applications, especially those that require more complex templates, using a **templating engine** can help organize your HTML generation. Templating engines like **Handlebars** or **Mustache** allow you to write reusable templates and then inject data into those templates.

For example, with Handlebars:

html

```
<script id="task-template" type="text/x-handlebars-
template">
    <ul>
        {{#each tasks}}
            <li>{{this}} <button class="remove-
btn">Remove</button></li>
        {{/each}}
    </ul>
</script>
```

You can then compile the template and inject data like this:

javascript

```
let templateSource = document.getElementById("task-
template").innerHTML;
let template = Handlebars.compile(templateSource);
let html = template({ tasks: tasks });
document.getElementById("taskList").innerHTML = html;
```

This approach separates the HTML structure from the JavaScript logic, making it easier to manage large applications with complex templates.

Assembling the Full To-Do App

Now that we've covered the core concepts, let's bring everything together to build our full **to-do tracker**. This application will:

1. Use **hash-based routing** to navigate between views (tasks, settings, etc.).
2. Maintain state in memory and in **localStorage** to persist tasks.
3. Dynamically render the task list using **manual templating**.
4. Handle task additions, removals, and completion.

Step 1: Setting Up the HTML

html

```
<div id="taskList"></div>
<button onclick="addTask(prompt('Enter task:'))">Add
Task</button>
```

Step 2: JavaScript for Task Management and Routing

javascript

```
let tasks = JSON.parse(localStorage.getItem('tasks'))
|| [];

function updateTaskList() {
    document.getElementById("taskList").innerHTML =
tasks.map(task => `<li>${task}</li>`).join('');
    localStorage.setItem('tasks',
JSON.stringify(tasks));
}

function addTask(task) {
    if (task) {
        tasks.push(task);
        updateTaskList();
    }
}

window.addEventListener("hashchange", () => {
    let hash = window.location.hash;
    if (hash === "#/tasks") {
        updateTaskList();
    }
});
```

Key Takeaways

In this chapter, we've covered the essentials of building a Single-Page Application:

1. **Client-side routing**: Implementing hash-based routing to navigate between different views without reloading the page.

2. **State management**: Keeping track of the application state (tasks) in memory and storing it in localStorage for persistence.

3. **Templating**: Dynamically rendering HTML based on data and updating the DOM to reflect changes in the state.

You now have a solid foundation for building interactive, dynamic web applications that don't require constant page reloads

Chapter 11: Testing and Tracing Bugs

As developers, one of the most critical skills we can master is debugging and testing. While it's inevitable that bugs will arise as we write code, having the tools and strategies to efficiently identify and fix these bugs can drastically improve the quality of our code, save time, and make our applications more robust.

In this chapter, we'll dive deep into two essential aspects of development: **debugging** and **testing**. We'll first explore the tools that can help us identify and fix bugs in our code, such as the Chrome Debugger and console logging. Then, we'll tackle the world of **unit testing**, specifically with **Jest**, a popular testing framework for JavaScript. We'll walk through the process of writing tests for an existing project (a **converter and inventory tracker**) to ensure that our code behaves as expected.

By the end of this chapter, you'll understand how to approach debugging and testing with confidence. You'll know how to break down complex issues, write tests that catch errors early, and use powerful tools like the Chrome Debugger and Jest to streamline the development process.

Debugging: The Art of Tracing Bugs

Every developer has faced the frustration of bugs in their code. Sometimes, the issue is obvious, but other times, the cause of the problem is elusive. Understanding how to effectively debug your code is key to overcoming these challenges.

In JavaScript, there are several tools and techniques you can use to trace bugs and errors. These include the **Chrome Debugger**, **console logging**, and other debugging utilities built into modern browsers.

1. Chrome Debugger: Step-by-Step Debugging

The **Chrome Developer Tools** (DevTools) are an essential part of debugging JavaScript in web applications. DevTools provide an interactive environment for inspecting your code, setting breakpoints, stepping through code line by line, and observing the behavior of your application in real-time.

To open Chrome DevTools, simply press `Ctrl + Shift + I` (or `Cmd + Option + I` on Mac) or right-click anywhere on the page and select **Inspect**. Once the DevTools panel is open, navigate to the **Sources** tab. Here, you'll find your JavaScript files, where you can set breakpoints and begin debugging.

2. Setting Breakpoints

A **breakpoint** is a marker you can place in your code to pause execution at a specific line. This allows you to inspect variables, evaluate expressions, and understand the flow of your code step by step.

To set a breakpoint in Chrome DevTools:

1. Open the **Sources** tab.
2. Navigate to the JavaScript file you want to debug.
3. Click on the line number where you want to set a breakpoint. A blue marker will appear, indicating the breakpoint.

Once the breakpoint is set, reload your page or trigger the code that runs your JavaScript. The execution will pause at the breakpoint, allowing you to inspect the current state of your variables and see where things might be going wrong.

3. Stepping Through Code

When the debugger hits a breakpoint, you have several options for how to proceed:

- **Step Over**: This moves the execution to the next line of code, skipping over any function calls.

- **Step Into**: If the current line contains a function call, this will step into that function and allow you to debug it line by line.
- **Step Out**: This will exit the current function and move to the next line in the calling function.
- **Resume Script Execution**: This continues the execution of your code until the next breakpoint is hit.

Using these options, you can navigate through your code and examine its state at any point during execution.

4. Inspecting Variables

One of the most powerful features of the Chrome Debugger is the ability to inspect variables during runtime. When the debugger pauses at a breakpoint, you can view the **Call Stack** (the series of function calls that led to the current point), the **Scope** (the local and global variables accessible at that point), and the **Watch Expressions** (custom variables you want to track).

In the **Scope** section, you'll see all the local variables and their current values. You can also add **watch expressions** to track specific variables or expressions as the code executes. This makes it easy to identify where things might be going wrong.

Console Logging: A Simple Yet Powerful Debugging Tool

While the Chrome Debugger is incredibly powerful, sometimes the simplest tools are the best. **Console logging** (using `console.log()`) is one of the most widely used methods for debugging JavaScript code. By logging values at different points in your program, you can trace the flow of data and identify issues.

1. Basic Console Logging

The most basic form of console logging is using `console.log()` to output values to the browser console:

```javascript
let age = 25;
console.log(age);   // Output: 25
```

You can log any variable, object, or expression to the console, making it easy to see what's going on in your code at any point.

2. Logging Objects and Arrays

Logging objects and arrays can help you inspect complex data structures. However, simply logging them as-is may not always provide clear insights, especially for large or deeply nested objects. Here are some techniques for better object and array logging:

- **console.table()**: This method displays arrays and objects in a table format, making them easier to read and compare.

javascript

```
let users = [{ name: "Alice", age: 30 }, { name:
"Bob", age: 25 }];
console.table(users);
```

- **console.dir()**: This method displays a more detailed, interactive view of objects, showing their properties and methods.

javascript

```
let person = { name: "Alice", age: 30 };
console.dir(person);
```

3. Debugging with `console.assert()`

`console.assert()` is another useful method for debugging. It allows you to log a message only if a specified condition is false:

javascript

```
let age = 25;
console.assert(age >= 18, "Age must be at least 18");
```

If the condition is false, the assertion will log the error message to the console. If it's true, nothing happens.

Unit Testing: Writing Tests to Ensure Code Quality

While debugging helps you identify and fix issues during development, **unit testing** helps ensure that your code behaves as expected over time. **Unit tests** are small, focused tests that check the functionality of individual parts of your code, such as functions or methods.

1. Why Write Tests?

- **Catch errors early**: Unit tests can help you identify bugs and errors before they make it into production.
- **Ensure code correctness**: Tests verify that your code produces the correct results for various inputs.
- **Facilitate refactoring**: When you make changes to your code, unit tests ensure that the functionality remains intact.
- **Documentation**: Tests serve as documentation for how your code is intended to behave.

2. Introduction to Jest

Jest is one of the most popular testing frameworks for JavaScript, and it's particularly well-suited for unit testing in modern JavaScript applications. It comes with built-in features like **mocking**, **spying**, and **asynchronous testing**. Additionally, Jest has great support for working with **React**, though it can be used with any JavaScript framework.

To get started with Jest, you first need to install it:

bash

```
npm install --save-dev jest
```

Once Jest is installed, you can run your tests with the following command:

bash

```
npx jest
```

3. Writing Simple Tests

Jest tests are written using **matchers** that check if a given value meets a specific condition. Here's an example of a simple unit test for a function that adds two numbers:

```javascript
// math.js
function add(a, b) {
    return a + b;
}

module.exports = add;
```

```javascript
// math.test.js
const add = require("./math");

test("adds 1 + 2 to equal 3", () => {
    expect(add(1, 2)).toBe(3);
});
```

In this example:

- We use the `test()` function to define a test case. The first argument is the test description, and the second argument is a callback function containing the actual test logic.
- `expect()` is used to specify what we expect the result to be, and `.toBe()` is a matcher that checks if the result is equal to the expected value.

4. Writing Tests for Our Converter and Inventory Tracker

Now let's write some tests for the converter and inventory tracker we've previously worked on. First, we'll test the **converter function**:

javascript

```javascript
// converter.js
function convertTemperature(celsius) {
    return (celsius * 9/5) + 32;
}

module.exports = convertTemperature;
```

javascript

```javascript
// converter.test.js
const convertTemperature = require("./converter");

test("converts Celsius to Fahrenheit", () => {
    expect(convertTemperature(0)).toBe(32);
    expect(convertTemperature(100)).toBe(212);
});
```

Next, we'll write tests for the **inventory tracker**:

javascript

```javascript
// inventory.js
let inventory = [];
```

```
function addItem(item) {
    inventory.push(item);
}

function getItemCount() {
    return inventory.length;
}

module.exports = { addItem, getItemCount };
javascript

// inventory.test.js
const { addItem, getItemCount } =
require("./inventory");

test("adds items to inventory", () => {
    addItem("Laptop");
    addItem("Phone");
    expect(getItemCount()).toBe(2);
});
```

5. Running Tests in Watch Mode

Jest has a great feature called **watch mode**, which allows you to run tests continuously as you make changes to your code. To start Jest in watch mode, simply run:

```bash
```

```
npx jest --watch
```

Watch mode will re-run your tests automatically whenever you save a file, making it easier to test and debug your code while developing.

Key Takeaways

In this chapter, you've learned how to debug and test your JavaScript code effectively. You now know how to use:

- **Chrome Debugger** to set breakpoints, step through code, and inspect variables.
- **Console logging** with advanced methods like `console.table()`, `console.dir()`, and `console.assert()` for better debugging.
- **Jest** to write unit tests for your code, ensuring that your functions behave as expected and catching bugs early.
- **Watch mode** in Jest to run tests continuously while you work, improving the development workflow.

By incorporating debugging and testing into your development process, you'll improve the reliability and maintainability of your applications.

Chapter 12: Automating Builds — npm, Bundlers & Transpilers

As web development evolves, so does the complexity of applications. When building modern web applications, it's crucial to manage code efficiently and ensure that it's optimized for performance and compatibility. One of the most important aspects of this process is automating your build pipeline. This allows you to streamline your development process, optimize your code, and ensure that your application runs smoothly across all environments.

In this chapter, we'll explore the tools that help us automate the build process: **npm**, **Babel**, and **Bundlers** like **webpack** or **rollup**. We'll cover how to use npm scripts for automation, how to configure Babel to ensure backward compatibility with older browsers, and how to use bundlers to package your modular code into a single optimized bundle.

By the end of this chapter, you'll have the knowledge to set up a build pipeline that compiles modern JavaScript into a format that works across all browsers, minifies your code to reduce file size, and makes your app production-ready.

What is a Build Pipeline?

A **build pipeline** is a series of automated steps that transform your raw code into an optimized, deployable product. It involves several processes, including:

1. **Transpiling**: Converting modern JavaScript (ES6+) into an older version that is compatible with older browsers.
2. **Bundling**: Combining multiple JavaScript files (or other assets like CSS and images) into a single file for easier deployment and improved performance.
3. **Minification**: Removing unnecessary characters (such as spaces and comments) from the code to reduce its size, making it load faster.
4. **Polyfills**: Adding missing features to older browsers so that they can run modern code smoothly.

The build pipeline ensures that your code is modular, backward-compatible, optimized for performance, and ready for deployment.

Configuring npm Scripts for Automation

At the core of many build systems lies **npm** (Node Package Manager). npm not only allows you to manage dependencies, but it also enables you to automate tasks via **npm scripts**. These scripts let you define custom commands that can run a series of tasks like testing, building, or serving your app.

1. Setting Up npm Scripts

You can define npm scripts in the `package.json` file, under the `"scripts"` section. For example:

json

```
{
  "name": "my-project",
  "version": "1.0.0",
  "scripts": {
    "start": "webpack serve",
    "build": "webpack --mode production",
    "test": "jest"
  }
}
```

In this example:

- The `"start"` script runs the development server using **webpack**.
- The `"build"` script bundles and optimizes the code for production using webpack.
- The `"test"` script runs tests with **Jest**.

You can run these scripts using the following command in the terminal:

```bash
bash
```

```bash
npm run build
```

2. Automating the Build Process

By using npm scripts, you can automate your entire build pipeline. Let's say you want to run multiple tasks, such as transpiling your code, bundling it, and minifying the output. You can chain tasks together like this:

```json
json

{
  "scripts": {
    "build": "npm run transpile && npm run bundle &&
npm run minify",
    "transpile": "babel src --out-dir dist",
    "bundle": "webpack --config webpack.config.js",
    "minify": "terser dist/main.js -o
dist/main.min.js"
  }
}
```

In this case:

- `"build"` runs three commands in sequence: transpiling, bundling, and minifying the code.
- `"transpile"` uses **Babel** to convert modern JavaScript into a backward-compatible version.
- `"bundle"` uses **webpack** to bundle your JavaScript code into a single file.
- `"minify"` uses **terser** to minify the bundled code, reducing its size.

This approach ensures that every time you run `npm run build`, your entire build process is executed automatically, producing an optimized production build.

Babel: Ensuring Backward Compatibility

Babel is a popular JavaScript transpiler that allows you to write modern JavaScript (ES6 and beyond) while ensuring backward compatibility with older browsers. It converts modern JavaScript code into an older version (e.g., ES5) that works across a wider range of browsers.

1. Setting Up Babel

To use Babel in your project, you need to install Babel and its dependencies. Start by installing the necessary packages:

```bash
bash
```

```bash
npm install --save-dev @babel/core @babel/cli
@babel/preset-env
```

- `@babel/core`: The main Babel package.
- `@babel/cli`: Allows you to run Babel from the command line.
- `@babel/preset-env`: A preset that compiles modern JavaScript down to a version compatible with the target browsers.

Next, create a `.babelrc` file in the root of your project to configure Babel. This file will specify the **preset** and the **targets** (the browsers you want to support).

```json
json
```

```json
{
  "presets": [
    ["@babel/preset-env", {
      "targets": "> 0.25%, not dead"
    }]
  ]
}
```

This configuration tells Babel to transpile JavaScript so it works in browsers that have more than 0.25% market share and are not officially deprecated.

2. Transpiling Code with Babel

To transpile your code with Babel, add an npm script to your `package.json` file:

json

```json
{
  "scripts": {
    "transpile": "babel src --out-dir dist"
  }
}
```

In this example, `babel src --out-dir dist` will transpile the files in the `src` directory and output them into the `dist` directory.

You can now run the following command to transpile your code:

bash

```bash
npm run transpile
```

Babel will process your code, ensuring it works across all supported browsers, even older ones that don't support ES6+ features like arrow functions, `let`/`const`, template literals, and more.

Bundlers: Combining Code into a Single File

As your application grows, managing multiple JavaScript files can become cumbersome. Instead of loading several separate files, it's more efficient to **bundle** your JavaScript code into a single file. This reduces the number of HTTP requests needed to load your app, improving performance.

Two popular bundlers are **webpack** and **rollup**. Both of these tools take your modular code and combine it into a single optimized bundle.

1. Using Webpack for Bundling

Webpack is the most widely used bundler in the JavaScript ecosystem. It takes modules (JavaScript files, images, CSS, etc.) and bundles them together into a single file (or multiple files, depending on your configuration).

Setting Up Webpack

To get started with webpack, you need to install it along with some additional plugins:

bash

```
npm install --save-dev webpack webpack-cli webpack-dev-server
```

You'll also need to create a `webpack.config.js` file that tells webpack how to bundle your files.

javascript

```javascript
const path = require("path");

module.exports = {
  entry: "./src/index.js", // Entry point of your application
  output: {
    filename: "bundle.js", // Name of the output file
    path: path.resolve(__dirname, "dist")
  },
  module: {
    rules: [
      {
        test: /\.js$/, // Apply Babel transpiling to JavaScript files
```

```
        exclude: /node_modules/,
        use: {
          loader: "babel-loader"
        }
      }
    ]
  },
  devServer: {
    contentBase: path.join(__dirname, "dist"),
    compress: true,
    port: 9000
  }
};
```

In this configuration:

- `entry` specifies the entry point of the application (where webpack starts bundling).
- `output` defines the output file and directory for the bundled code.
- `module.rules` defines how to process files (in this case, using Babel to transpile JavaScript).
- `devServer` sets up a local development server for testing the app.

To build your project, run the following command:

```bash
bash
```

```
npx webpack --config webpack.config.js
```

This will generate a bundled file called `bundle.js` in the `dist` directory.

2. Using Rollup for Bundling

Rollup is another bundler that's optimized for bundling JavaScript libraries and smaller apps. It's known for producing smaller, more efficient bundles compared to webpack.

Setting Up Rollup

To set up Rollup, install it via npm:

```bash
```

```
npm install --save-dev rollup
```

Next, create a `rollup.config.js` file to configure Rollup:

```javascript
```

```
export default {
    input: "src/index.js",
    output: {
        file: "dist/bundle.js",
        format: "iife"
```

```
    }
};
```

This configuration tells Rollup to bundle your code starting from `src/index.js` and output it to `dist/bundle.js` in the **IIFE** (Immediately Invoked Function Expression) format.

To build your project with Rollup, run:

```bash
npx rollup -c
```

Rollup will produce a single bundled file in the `dist` directory.

Minification: Reducing File Size

Once your code is bundled, it's a good idea to **minify** it. Minification removes unnecessary characters (like spaces, line breaks, and comments) from your code, reducing its file size and improving load times.

1. Minifying Code with Terser

Terser is a popular JavaScript minifier. To use it, install it via npm:

```bash
npm install --save-dev terser
```

You can integrate Terser into your build process with npm scripts:

```json
{
  "scripts": {
    "minify": "terser dist/bundle.js -o
dist/bundle.min.js"
  }
}
```

Run the following command to minify your code:

```bash
npm run minify
```

Terser will generate a minified version of your code, reducing its size and making it ready for production.

Polyfills: Ensuring Compatibility

As JavaScript evolves, new features are introduced that aren't supported by all browsers, especially older ones. **Polyfills** are pieces of code that provide functionality for newer JavaScript features in older browsers.

For example, older browsers may not support `Array.prototype.includes`, so you can use a polyfill to make that method available.

1. Adding Polyfills with Babel

Babel can automatically add polyfills to your code based on the browser support you need. To enable this feature, you'll need to install `@babel/preset-env` and the **core-js** library.

bash

```
npm install --save-dev @babel/preset-env core-js
```

Next, update your `.babelrc` file to include the `useBuiltIns` option:

json

```
{
  "presets": [
    [
```

```
    "@babel/preset-env",
    {
      "useBuiltIns": "usage",
      "corejs": 3
    }
  ]
  ]
}
```

This configuration ensures that Babel automatically adds only the necessary polyfills for the features your code uses, based on your target browsers.

Key Takeaways

In this chapter, we've explored the process of **automating builds** and optimizing JavaScript for modern applications:

1. **npm scripts**: Automate tasks like transpiling, bundling, and minification, saving time and improving efficiency.
2. **Babel**: Ensure compatibility with older browsers by transpiling modern JavaScript into a backward-compatible version.
3. **Bundlers (webpack and rollup)**: Combine multiple JavaScript files into a single file, improving performance and reducing the number of HTTP requests.

4. **Minification**: Reduce the file size of your bundled code to improve loading times and performance.
5. **Polyfills**: Ensure compatibility with older browsers by automatically adding necessary polyfills.

By setting up a proper build pipeline, you can ensure that your code is production-ready and optimized for all browsers, while maintaining a smooth development workflow

Chapter 13: JavaScript on the Server — Node.js & Express

For a long time, JavaScript was known primarily for being a client-side language, running in the browser to create dynamic, interactive web pages. However, with the advent of **Node.js**, JavaScript made its way to the server-side as well, allowing developers to use the same language for both the front end and back end. This has resulted in a unified and efficient development experience.

In this chapter, we'll explore **Node.js** and **Express**, two powerful tools that allow you to build fast, scalable, and highly maintainable web applications on the server-side. We'll walk through how to set up an **Express server**, define **routes**, create **middleware**, and serve **static files**. Then, we'll use these concepts to build a **REST API** for an inventory app, implementing **CRUD (Create, Read, Update, Delete)** endpoints.

By the end of this chapter, you'll have a solid understanding of how to set up a server, handle requests, and build an API that can serve data to clients, all using JavaScript.

Understanding Node.js: JavaScript on the Server

Before we dive into Express, it's important to understand **Node.js**. Node.js is a **runtime environment** that allows JavaScript to be executed outside of the browser. It uses **V8**, the JavaScript engine developed by Google, to execute code. Node.js is built on a non-blocking, event-driven architecture, which makes it highly efficient for building scalable network applications.

Key Features of Node.js:

1. **Non-blocking, asynchronous I/O**: Node.js can handle many requests simultaneously without waiting for each to complete before starting the next one. This makes it ideal for applications that require high throughput, like APIs and real-time applications.

2. **Single-threaded**: Unlike traditional server-side languages like Java or PHP, which spawn multiple threads to handle requests, Node.js runs on a single thread, using **event loops** to manage asynchronous operations.

3. **NPM (Node Package Manager)**: NPM allows you to install, manage, and share packages (libraries or modules) that make development in Node.js easier. It's the largest ecosystem of open-source libraries in the world.

Setting Up Node.js and Express

To build a server with Node.js and Express, we first need to install **Node.js**. You can download it from the official website: <u>nodejs.org</u>.

Once Node.js is installed, you'll also have access to `npm`, which you'll use to manage dependencies (libraries and packages) for your project.

1. Initialize a Node.js Project

The first step in any Node.js project is to initialize it with `npm`. This creates a `package.json` file, which will keep track of your project's dependencies, scripts, and metadata.

Run the following command in your terminal:

```bash

npm init -y
```

The `-y` flag automatically fills in default values for the project setup. If you prefer to configure it manually, omit the `-y` flag, and npm will prompt you for details such as the project name, version, and description.

2. Installing Express

Next, install **Express,** a minimal and flexible web application framework for Node.js. Express simplifies routing, middleware handling, and other server-side tasks, allowing you to focus on building your application.

Install Express using npm:

```bash
bash
```

```bash
npm install express
```

This will add Express to your `node_modules` folder and update the `package.json` file to include Express as a dependency.

3. Setting Up an Express Server

Now that we've installed Express, let's set up a simple Express server. Create a file called `server.js`:

```javascript
javascript
```

```javascript
// Import the express module
const express = require('express');

// Create an instance of the Express app
const app = express();
```

```
// Define a basic route
app.get('/', (req, res) => {
    res.send('Hello, world!');
});

// Start the server and listen on a port
const port = 3000;
app.listen(port, () => {
    console.log(`Server running at
http://localhost:${port}`);
});
```

In this example:

- We import Express using `require('express')`.
- We create an Express app instance using `express()`.
- We define a route for the root URL (/) using `app.get()`, which responds with "Hello, world!".
- Finally, we start the server on port 3000 and log a message when the server is up and running.

Run the server with the following command:

```bash
```

```
node server.js
```

Navigate to `http://localhost:3000` in your browser, and you should see the message "Hello, world!" displayed.

Understanding Routes in Express

Routes are the backbone of any web application. In Express, routes define how your server will respond to different HTTP requests. You can define routes for different HTTP methods, such as **GET**, **POST**, **PUT**, and **DELETE**, and map them to specific URL paths.

1. Defining Routes

Here's an example of defining multiple routes in Express:

javascript

```
app.get('/home', (req, res) => {
    res.send('Welcome to the home page!');
});

app.post('/submit', (req, res) => {
    res.send('Form submitted successfully!');
});

app.put('/update/:id', (req, res) => {
    res.send(`Updating item with ID:
${req.params.id}`);
```

```
});

app.delete('/delete/:id', (req, res) => {
    res.send(`Deleting item with ID:
${req.params.id}`);
});
```

In this example:

- **GET /home**: Responds to a GET request at the `/home` URL.
- **POST /submit**: Responds to a POST request at the `/submit` URL.
- **PUT /update/:id**: Responds to a PUT request at `/update/:id`, where `:id` is a dynamic parameter.
- **DELETE /delete/:id**: Responds to a DELETE request at `/delete/:id`.

2. Route Parameters

In Express, you can define **route parameters** by prefixing the parameter name with a colon (`:`). For example, in the route `app.get('/user/:id')`, `id` is a parameter, and you can access it using `req.params.id`.

3. Query Parameters

You can also pass query parameters in the URL. For example, a URL like `/search?term=express` would include the `term` query parameter. In Express, you can access query parameters using `req.query`.

```javascript
app.get('/search', (req, res) => {
    const term = req.query.term;
    res.send(`Searching for: ${term}`);
});
```

Middleware: Functions That Modify Requests and Responses

Middleware in Express is a powerful feature that allows you to modify requests and responses as they travel through the server. Middleware functions have access to the `req` and `res` objects, and they can perform actions such as logging, authentication, data validation, or modifying the response before it's sent to the client.

1. Using Built-in Middleware

Express comes with several built-in middleware functions. For example, the `express.json()` middleware automatically parses incoming JSON payloads:

javascript

```javascript
app.use(express.json());
```

This line of code tells Express to use the `express.json()` middleware for all incoming requests. This is essential when working with APIs that accept JSON data in the request body.

2. Custom Middleware

You can also write your own middleware to handle custom functionality. Here's an example of a simple middleware function that logs the request method and URL:

javascript

```javascript
function logRequest(req, res, next) {
    console.log(`${req.method} ${req.url}`);
    next(); // Pass the request to the next
middleware or route handler
}
```

```
app.use(logRequest);
```

In this example:

- The `logRequest` middleware logs the HTTP method (`req.method`) and the URL (`req.url`).
- The `next()` function passes control to the next middleware or route handler.

3. Error Handling Middleware

Express provides a way to handle errors using **error-handling middleware**. This middleware is defined with four arguments: `err`, `req`, `res`, and `next`.

Here's an example of error-handling middleware:

javascript

```javascript
function errorHandler(err, req, res, next) {
    console.error(err.stack);
    res.status(500).send('Something went wrong!');
}

app.use(errorHandler);
```

This middleware catches errors in the application and sends a 500 response with the message "Something went wrong!".

Serving Static Files

In many web applications, you'll need to serve static files like HTML, CSS, JavaScript, and images. Express provides a built-in middleware called `express.static()` that makes it easy to serve static files.

Serving Static Files

You can serve static files from a specific directory using the `express.static()` middleware. Here's how you can serve files from a `public` folder:

```javascript
app.use(express.static('public'));
```

Now, any file placed in the `public` directory (like `public/index.html`) will be accessible via the browser. For example, if you have an image file at `public/images/logo.png`, it can be accessed at `http://localhost:3000/images/logo.png`.

Building a REST API for the Inventory App

Let's now build a simple **REST API** for the inventory app. This API will include **CRUD (Create, Read, Update, Delete)** endpoints to manage products in the inventory.

1. Define Routes for CRUD Operations

Here's how you might define the routes for managing the inventory:

javascript

```javascript
let inventory = [
    { id: 1, name: 'Laptop', quantity: 10 },
    { id: 2, name: 'Phone', quantity: 5 }
];

app.get('/api/products', (req, res) => {
    res.json(inventory);
});

app.get('/api/products/:id', (req, res) => {
    const product = inventory.find(p => p.id ===
parseInt(req.params.id));
    if (product) {
        res.json(product);
    } else {
        res.status(404).send('Product not found');
    }
```

```
});

app.post('/api/products', (req, res) => {
    const newProduct = req.body;
    newProduct.id = inventory.length + 1;
    inventory.push(newProduct);
    res.status(201).json(newProduct);
});

app.put('/api/products/:id', (req, res) => {
    const product = inventory.find(p => p.id ===
parseInt(req.params.id));
    if (product) {
        product.name = req.body.name;
        product.quantity = req.body.quantity;
        res.json(product);
    } else {
        res.status(404).send('Product not found');
    }
});

app.delete('/api/products/:id', (req, res) => {
    const productIndex = inventory.findIndex(p =>
p.id === parseInt(req.params.id));
    if (productIndex !== -1) {
        inventory.splice(productIndex, 1);
        res.status(204).send();
    } else {
        res.status(404).send('Product not found');
```

```
    }
});
```

In this example:

- **GET /api/products**: Fetches the list of products.
- **GET /api/products/:id**: Fetches a single product by its ID.
- **POST /api/products**: Adds a new product to the inventory.
- **PUT /api/products/:id**: Updates an existing product.
- **DELETE /api/products/:id**: Deletes a product by its ID.

2. Handling JSON Payloads

When dealing with JSON payloads, it's essential to use **middleware** that parses the incoming request body. In Express, this is done with `express.json()`:

javascript

```javascript
app.use(express.json());   // Enable JSON parsing
```

This middleware allows you to access the request body as a JavaScript object using `req.body`. For example, in the `POST` and `PUT` routes, `req.body` contains the product data sent by the client.

Key Takeaways

In this chapter, you learned how to set up an **Express server**, handle different types of **HTTP requests**, and use **middleware** to manage requests, errors, and static files. We built a simple **REST API** for an inventory app with CRUD operations, demonstrating how to:

- Set up an Express server and define routes for different HTTP methods.
- Handle JSON payloads and use middleware to process incoming requests.
- Serve static files and create error-handling middleware.
- Build a REST API for managing products, including creating, reading, updating, and deleting data.

Express is a powerful framework for building server-side applications with JavaScript, and combined with Node.js, it opens up endless possibilities for creating dynamic, scalable web applications.

Chapter 14: Splitting into Microservices

As web applications grow in complexity, maintaining a monolithic architecture—where everything is housed in a single, massive codebase—becomes increasingly difficult. Code tends to get bloated, testing and deployment processes become cumbersome, and scaling the application to meet demand can be challenging. **Microservices** offer a solution by breaking down a large application into smaller, manageable pieces, each with its own responsibility. This approach allows for greater flexibility, scalability, and maintainability.

In this chapter, we'll explore the concept of microservices and learn how to split a monolithic application into **microservices**. We'll specifically use **Node.js** with **Express** to build and deploy multiple small applications that handle specific functionality (such as **user authentication**, **inventory management**, and **order processing**). Each service will have its own database or data store, and we'll explore how these services communicate with each other efficiently.

By the end of this chapter, you'll be equipped with the knowledge to design and implement a microservices architecture, allowing you to divide your application into focused, independent services that are easier to scale and maintain.

What Are Microservices?

Microservices is an architectural style where an application is composed of a collection of **small, independent services**, each responsible for a specific business function. These services communicate with each other over standard protocols, like HTTP or messaging queues. Each service is built around a single responsibility, which makes it easier to maintain, test, and scale.

Characteristics of Microservices:

1. **Single Responsibility**: Each microservice is designed to handle a single function or business capability.
2. **Independence**: Microservices operate independently from each other, meaning each service can be developed, deployed, and scaled individually.
3. **Distributed**: Microservices communicate over the network, typically using RESTful APIs or messaging systems.
4. **Decentralized Data Management**: Each microservice typically has its own database or data store, reducing the need for shared databases and centralized data models.

5. **Failure Isolation**: A failure in one microservice does not necessarily affect other services, allowing for more resilient systems.

6. **Independent Scaling**: Services can be scaled independently based on load, making the application more flexible.

Why Microservices?

Traditional monolithic applications often struggle with scalability, flexibility, and maintainability as they grow. In contrast, microservices offer several advantages:

1. **Easier to Scale**: Microservices can be scaled independently, meaning you can scale only the services that need more resources.

2. **Faster Development and Deployment**: Teams can work on different services concurrently, improving the speed of development and enabling more frequent releases.

3. **Resilience and Fault Isolation**: If one service fails, it doesn't take down the entire system, reducing downtime.

4. **Flexibility in Technology Stack**: Each service can be built using the most appropriate technology for its specific task. For instance, you might use **Node.js** for the user authentication service and **Python** for data analytics.

5. **Simpler Maintenance**: Since services are smaller and focused, it's easier to maintain and update them without affecting the entire application.

The Challenges of Microservices

While microservices offer many benefits, they come with their own set of challenges, including:

1. **Increased Complexity**: Managing many small services increases the complexity of the system as a whole.
2. **Inter-Service Communication**: Services need to communicate with each other, and managing these communications efficiently can be tricky.
3. **Data Consistency**: Each microservice manages its own data, so ensuring consistency across services can be challenging, especially when dealing with distributed systems.
4. **Deployment Overhead**: Deploying many independent services can introduce overhead in terms of monitoring, deployment, and coordination.

Despite these challenges, microservices are an excellent solution for large applications that require scalability, flexibility, and maintainability.

Building Microservices with Express

In this section, we'll break down the steps to implement a microservices architecture using **Node.js** and **Express**. We'll build a simple system consisting of three microservices: one for **user authentication**, one for **inventory management**, and one for **order processing**.

Each microservice will be a separate Express app with its own database or data store. These services will communicate with each other through **RESTful APIs**.

1. Setting Up the Project

To start, let's create a project folder and initialize it with `npm`:

bash

```
mkdir microservices-example
cd microservices-example
npm init -y
```

Next, let's install the required dependencies:

bash

```
npm install express mongoose body-parser
```

Here, we've installed **Express** for building the server, **Mongoose** for interacting with MongoDB (we'll use MongoDB as our data store), and **Body-parser** to parse incoming request bodies.

Microservice 1: User Authentication Service

The first service we'll build is a **User Authentication Service**. This service will handle user registration, login, and token generation using **JWT** (JSON Web Tokens).

1. Define the User Model

Create a folder called `auth-service`:

bash

```
mkdir auth-service
cd auth-service
```

Inside this folder, create a file called `userModel.js` to define the **User schema**:

```javascript
const mongoose = require('mongoose');

const userSchema = new mongoose.Schema({
    username: { type: String, required: true, unique: true },
    password: { type: String, required: true },
});

const User = mongoose.model('User', userSchema);

module.exports = User;
```

2. User Registration and Login Routes

Now, let's create the **registration** and **login** routes in authService.js:

```javascript
const express = require('express');
const bodyParser = require('body-parser');
const mongoose = require('mongoose');
const User = require('./userModel');
const jwt = require('jsonwebtoken');

const app = express();
app.use(bodyParser.json());
```

```
mongoose.connect('mongodb://localhost:27017/authServi
ce', {
    useNewUrlParser: true,
    useUnifiedTopology: true,
});

app.post('/register', async (req, res) => {
    const { username, password } = req.body;

    const existingUser = await User.findOne({
username });
    if (existingUser) {
        return res.status(400).send('User already
exists');
    }

    const user = new User({ username, password });
    await user.save();
    res.status(201).send('User registered
successfully');
});

app.post('/login', async (req, res) => {
    const { username, password } = req.body;

    const user = await User.findOne({ username });
    if (!user || user.password !== password) {
        return res.status(400).send('Invalid username
or password');
```

```
    }

    const token = jwt.sign({ userId: user._id },
'secret', { expiresIn: '1h' });
    res.json({ token });
});

app.listen(3001, () => {
    console.log('User Authentication Service running
on port 3001');
});
```

3. Connecting to the User Authentication Service

Now that the authentication service is set up, we'll need to connect it with the other microservices. The order and inventory services will communicate with the user service to validate users before they can place orders or view inventory.

Microservice 2: Inventory Management Service

The second microservice we'll build is an **Inventory Management Service**. This service will handle the list of items in the inventory, including adding new items, updating item quantities, and retrieving items.

1. Define the Inventory Model

Create a folder called `inventory-service` and define the inventory model in `inventoryModel.js`:

javascript

```javascript
const mongoose = require('mongoose');

const inventorySchema = new mongoose.Schema({
    name: { type: String, required: true },
    quantity: { type: Number, required: true },
});

const Inventory = mongoose.model('Inventory',
inventorySchema);

module.exports = Inventory;
```

2. Inventory CRUD Routes

Create the routes for managing inventory in `inventoryService.js`:

javascript

```javascript
const express = require('express');
const bodyParser = require('body-parser');
const mongoose = require('mongoose');
const Inventory = require('./inventoryModel');
```

```
const app = express();
app.use(bodyParser.json());

mongoose.connect('mongodb://localhost:27017/inventory
Service', {
    useNewUrlParser: true,
    useUnifiedTopology: true,
});

app.post('/add', async (req, res) => {
    const { name, quantity } = req.body;
    const newItem = new Inventory({ name, quantity
});
    await newItem.save();
    res.status(201).send('Item added successfully');
});

app.get('/items', async (req, res) => {
    const items = await Inventory.find();
    res.json(items);
});

app.put('/update/:id', async (req, res) => {
    const { id } = req.params;
    const { name, quantity } = req.body;

    const item = await
Inventory.findByIdAndUpdate(id, { name, quantity }, {
new: true });
```

```
    if (!item) {
        return res.status(404).send('Item not
found');
    }

    res.json(item);
});

app.listen(3002, () => {
    console.log('Inventory Management Service running
on port 3002');
});
```

Microservice 3: Order Processing Service

The third microservice is the **Order Processing Service**. This service will handle customer orders, including creating new orders and viewing order details.

1. Define the Order Model

In the `order-service` folder, create `orderModel.js`:

javascript

```
const mongoose = require('mongoose');

const orderSchema = new mongoose.Schema({
```

```
    customerId: { type:
mongoose.Schema.Types.ObjectId, required: true },
    productId: { type:
mongoose.Schema.Types.ObjectId, required: true },
    quantity: { type: Number, required: true },
    status: { type: String, default: 'pending' },
});


const Order = mongoose.model('Order', orderSchema);


module.exports = Order;
```

2. Order CRUD Routes

Now, define the routes for managing orders in `orderService.js`:

javascript

```
const express = require('express');
const bodyParser = require('body-parser');
const mongoose = require('mongoose');
const Order = require('./orderModel');


const app = express();
app.use(bodyParser.json());


mongoose.connect('mongodb://localhost:27017/orderServ
ice', {
    useNewUrlParser: true,
    useUnifiedTopology: true,
```

```
});

app.post('/create', async (req, res) => {
    const { customerId, productId, quantity } =
req.body;
    const newOrder = new Order({ customerId,
productId, quantity });
    await newOrder.save();
    res.status(201).send('Order created
successfully');
});

app.get('/orders', async (req, res) => {
    const orders = await Order.find();
    res.json(orders);
});

app.listen(3003, () => {
    console.log('Order Processing Service running on
port 3003');
});
```

Inter-Service Communication: How Services Talk to Each Other

One of the primary challenges of microservices is how different services communicate with each other. Since each service is independent and runs in its own process, they need a way to exchange data.

In our example, the **Order Processing Service** will need to interact with both the **User Authentication Service** and the **Inventory Management Service**:

- **User Authentication Service**: Verifies that the user is authenticated before they can place an order.
- **Inventory Management Service**: Ensures that there is enough stock available before processing an order.

The most common way microservices communicate is through **RESTful APIs**. Services send HTTP requests (usually `GET`, `POST`, `PUT`, `DELETE`) to each other to exchange data.

1. Making HTTP Requests Between Services

In our **Order Processing Service**, we can use the `axios` library to make HTTP requests to other services. For example, before processing an order, we can verify the user's authentication by calling the **User Authentication Service** API:

javascript

```javascript
const axios = require('axios');
```

```javascript
async function checkUserAuthentication(token) {
    try {
        const response = await
axios.get('http://localhost:3001/verify', {
            headers: { Authorization: `Bearer
${token}` },
        });
        return response.data; // User is
authenticated
    } catch (error) {
        throw new Error('Authentication failed');
    }
}
```

Similarly, we can check the **Inventory Management Service** for product availability:

javascript

```javascript
async function checkInventory(productId, quantity) {
    try {
        const response = await
axios.get(`http://localhost:3002/items/${productId}`)
;
        const item = response.data;
        if (item.quantity >= quantity) {
            return true; // Enough stock available
        } else {
            throw new Error('Not enough stock');
```

```
        }
    } catch (error) {
        throw new Error('Inventory check failed');
    }
}
```

Conclusion

In this chapter, you've learned how to break down a monolithic application into **microservices** using **Node.js** and **Express**. We've built three services that handle different parts of an application: **user authentication, inventory management**, and **order processing**.

We covered the following key concepts:

1. **Microservices architecture**: Breaking down functionality into small, focused services.
2. **Express**: Building lightweight web servers to handle HTTP requests and serve data.
3. **Inter-service communication**: Services communicate with each other through RESTful APIs, enabling them to work together while remaining independent.
4. **Handling different data stores**: Each service manages its own database or data store, reducing dependencies and improving scalability.

5. **CRUD operations**: Implementing basic create, read, update, and delete functionality for each service.

Microservices offer a scalable and maintainable approach to building web applications. While there are challenges, such as managing inter-service communication and handling data consistency, the benefits of flexibility, resilience, and scalability often outweigh the drawbacks.

Chapter 15: Deploying and Running in Production

Once you've built your application, whether it's a microservice-based system, a single-page application, or a backend API, it's time to deploy it. But deploying an app isn't just about putting it live on a server; it's about doing it in a way that is reliable, efficient, and scalable. In this chapter, we'll dive into the process of deploying and managing your applications in production using **modern deployment techniques**.

We'll cover the essentials, including **containerization** with **Docker**, deploying your app to popular platforms like **Heroku**, **AWS**, and **GitHub Actions**, and setting up a **continuous deployment pipeline**. Finally, we'll take a look at **monitoring**, **logging**, and **performance tuning** to ensure your app runs smoothly once it's live.

By the end of this chapter, you will have a robust, automated deployment pipeline that builds, tests, and deploys your application with minimal manual intervention. You'll also have the knowledge to ensure your application is well-monitored and tuned for production.

Understanding the Deployment Process

Deploying a web application into production involves several steps:

1. **Build**: This involves preparing your codebase by running tests, transpiling, bundling, and minifying it.
2. **Test**: You run automated tests to make sure your code works as expected.
3. **Deploy**: You push your application to a live environment, such as a cloud provider or a server.
4. **Monitor**: After deployment, you need to keep an eye on your app to ensure it's running as expected.
5. **Scale**: As traffic grows, you may need to scale your app horizontally (adding more instances) or vertically (adding more resources to existing instances).

Effective deployment ensures that your app is delivered with minimal downtime and maximum reliability. Automated deployment pipelines make the process repeatable and less error-prone, which is crucial when you deploy frequently.

Containerizing with Docker

Docker is a powerful tool for containerization, which allows you to package your application and all of its dependencies into a

container. A container is a lightweight, standalone, executable package that includes everything needed to run the app—such as the code, runtime, system tools, libraries, and settings—without worrying about environment-specific differences.

1. What is Docker?

Docker allows developers to package their applications into **Docker images**, which can then be run as **containers**. Containers are isolated from the host system and from each other, making it easier to deploy and scale applications in any environment, whether it's on a local machine, on a cloud server, or in a Kubernetes cluster.

2. Why Use Docker?

- **Consistency**: With Docker, you can be sure your app will work the same in development, staging, and production.
- **Portability**: Since Docker packages everything your app needs to run, you can run it anywhere Docker is supported, whether it's on a developer's laptop or in the cloud.
- **Isolation**: Each container runs independently, so your app's components can be isolated from one another, preventing issues caused by conflicting dependencies.
- **Scalability**: Docker makes it easier to scale your application by running multiple instances of your containers.

3. Setting Up Docker for Your Application

The first step in Dockerizing your application is to create a
Dockerfile, which defines how your app will be built into a container.
Here's a simple Dockerfile for a Node.js app:

```dockerfile
dockerfile

# Use the official Node.js image as a base
FROM node:14

# Set the working directory inside the container
WORKDIR /usr/src/app

#  package.json and package-lock.json
 package*.json ./

# Install the dependencies
RUN npm install

#  the rest of the application code
 . .

# Expose the port your app runs on
EXPOSE 3000

# Start the app
CMD ["npm", "start"]
```

This `Dockerfile`:

1. Starts from an official Node.js image (`node:14`).
2. Sets the working directory inside the container.
3. Installs the app's dependencies.
4. Copies the application code into the container.
5. Exposes the port that the app will run on (in this case, `3000`).
6. Defines the command to run the app.

To build the Docker image, use the following command:

```bash
docker build -t my-app .
```

Once the image is built, you can run your app in a container:

```bash
docker run -p 3000:3000 my-app
```

Now, your app is running inside a container and accessible on port 3000.

Deploying to Heroku

Heroku is a popular cloud platform that allows developers to deploy applications quickly without worrying about infrastructure. Heroku supports a variety of languages, including Node.js, and integrates well with Git, making it easy to deploy your application with a few simple commands.

1. Setting Up Heroku

To deploy your app to Heroku, you need to install the Heroku CLI (Command Line Interface) on your local machine. After installation, you can log in to your Heroku account:

bash

```
heroku login
```

2. Preparing for Deployment

To deploy your application to Heroku, first, you need to initialize a Git repository in your project directory (if you haven't already):

bash

```
git init
```

Then, add all the files to the repository:

```bash

git add .
git commit -m "Initial commit"
```

Next, create a new Heroku app:

```bash

heroku create my-app-name
```

This will create a new Heroku application and give you a URL where your app will be hosted.

3. Deploying the App

To deploy your app, push it to Heroku using Git:

```bash

git push heroku master
```

Heroku will automatically detect that you are deploying a Node.js app, install dependencies, and start the app.

4. Managing and Scaling on Heroku

Once your app is deployed, you can view it by running:

```bash
heroku open
```

To scale your app and manage resources, you can use the Heroku dashboard or the command line. For example, to increase the number of web dynos (instances of your app), run:

```bash
heroku ps:scale web=2
```

This will scale your app to run two instances (dynos) of your application, which can help handle more traffic.

Deploying to AWS with EC2

AWS (Amazon Web Services) is one of the most widely used cloud computing platforms. Using AWS, you can host your application on **EC2 (Elastic Compute Cloud)** instances, which are virtual servers in the cloud.

1. Setting Up an EC2 Instance

To deploy your app to AWS, start by creating an EC2 instance. You can do this via the AWS Management Console:

1. Go to the **EC2 Dashboard** and click **Launch Instance**.
2. Choose an **Amazon Machine Image (AMI)** (we'll use an Ubuntu image for this example).
3. Select an instance type (e.g., t2.micro for testing purposes).
4. Configure the instance settings and add a key pair for SSH access.

2. SSH into Your EC2 Instance

After the instance is created, you can SSH into it using the following command (replace `path/to/key.pem` with your actual key file and `ec2-user@your-ec2-ip` with your EC2 instance's public IP):

bash

```bash
ssh -i path/to/key.pem ec2-user@your-ec2-ip
```

3. Installing Dependencies on the EC2 Instance

Once inside the EC2 instance, install **Node.js** and any dependencies your application needs:

bash

```bash
sudo apt update
sudo apt install nodejs npm
```

Next, clone your repository or upload your application code to the EC2 instance.

4. Running Your App on EC2

To run your app, navigate to your project folder and install the necessary dependencies:

bash

```
npm install
```

Then, start your application:

bash

```
npm start
```

5. Setting Up a Reverse Proxy with Nginx

To make your app accessible on the web, you can set up a reverse proxy using **Nginx**. Install Nginx on the EC2 instance:

bash

```
sudo apt install nginx
```

Configure Nginx to forward requests to your Node.js app by editing the Nginx configuration file:

```bash
sudo nano /etc/nginx/sites-available/default
```

Add the following configuration to the `server` block:

```nginx
server {
    listen 80;
    server_name your-ec2-ip;

    location / {
        proxy_pass http://localhost:3000;
        proxy_http_version 1.1;
        proxy_set_header Upgrade $http_upgrade;
        proxy_set_header Connection 'upgrade';
        proxy_set_header Host $host;
        proxy_cache_bypass $http_upgrade;
    }
}
```

After updating the configuration, restart Nginx:

```bash
sudo systemctl restart nginx
```

Your app should now be accessible on your EC2 instance's public IP.

Setting Up a Continuous Deployment Pipeline with GitHub Actions

GitHub Actions is a powerful automation tool that integrates directly with GitHub repositories. It allows you to set up a continuous integration (CI) and continuous deployment (CD) pipeline to automate tasks like running tests, building your app, and deploying it.

1. Setting Up GitHub Actions

In your GitHub repository, create a folder called `.github/workflows` and inside that folder, create a file called `deploy.yml`:

```yaml
yaml

name: Deploy to Heroku

on:
  push:
    branches:
      - main

jobs:
  build:
```

```
   runs-on: ubuntu-latest

  steps:
    - name: Checkout code
      uses: actions/checkout@v2

    - name: Set up Node.js
      uses: actions/setup-node@v2
      with:
        node-version: '14'

    - name: Install dependencies
      run: npm install

    - name: Run tests
      run: npm test

    - name: Deploy to Heroku
      uses: akshnz/heroku-deploy-action@v2.0.0
      with:
        heroku_api_key: ${{ secrets.HEROKU_API_KEY
}}
        heroku_app_name: your-heroku-app-name
        heroku_email: your-heroku-email@example.com
```

This configuration tells GitHub Actions to:

1. Trigger the pipeline whenever changes are pushed to the
    `main` branch.

2. Set up Node.js, install dependencies, and run tests.

3. Deploy the app to **Heroku** (or any other platform of your choice).

2. Set Up Secrets

For security purposes, store sensitive information like your Heroku API key and email in **GitHub secrets**. Go to your GitHub repository's settings, and under the **Secrets** section, add the necessary secrets (`HEROKU_API_KEY`, `HEROKU_EMAIL`).

Monitoring and Performance Tuning

Once your app is live, you need to ensure it runs smoothly. This involves setting up **monitoring**, tracking **logs**, and performing **performance tuning**.

1. Logging

Logging is crucial for diagnosing issues and understanding your app's behavior. **Winston** is a popular logging library in Node.js that allows you to log information at different levels (info, warn, error).

Install Winston:

```bash
```

```
npm install winston
```

Configure Winston to log to the console and a file:

```
javascript
```

```javascript
const winston = require('winston');

const logger = winston.createLogger({
    level: 'info',
    transports: [
        new winston.transports.Console(),
        new winston.transports.File({ filename:
'app.log' })
    ]
});
```

Now, you can log messages throughout your app:

```
javascript
```

```javascript
logger.info('App started');
logger.error('An error occurred');
```

2. Monitoring

PM2 is a process manager for Node.js that helps keep your app running smoothly in production. It also offers built-in monitoring and logging features.

To install PM2:

bash

```
npm install pm2 -g
```

Start your app with PM2:

bash

```
pm2 start server.js
```

PM2 will keep your app running in the background, and you can use the following command to monitor its status:

bash

```
pm2 monit
```

3. Performance Tuning

Performance tuning involves optimizing your app to handle more traffic and reduce latency. Some common techniques include:

- **Caching**: Cache frequently accessed data to reduce database load and improve response times.
- **Load balancing**: Distribute traffic across multiple instances of your app to prevent bottlenecks.

- **Database optimization**: Use indexes and optimize queries to ensure your database can handle large amounts of data efficiently.
- **Lazy loading**: Only load resources when they are needed, reducing the initial load time.

Key Takeaways

In this chapter, you've learned how to deploy and manage your application in a production environment. We covered:

1. **Containerization with Docker**: Packaging your application into containers to ensure consistency across environments.
2. **Deploying to Heroku and AWS**: Setting up cloud deployment for scalable, reliable applications.
3. **Continuous Deployment with GitHub Actions**: Automating your deployment pipeline with CI/CD tools.
4. **Monitoring and Logging**: Setting up logging and monitoring to ensure your application runs smoothly in production.
5. **Performance Tuning**: Implementing strategies like caching, load balancing, and database optimization to improve your app's performance.

With these skills, you can confidently deploy, monitor, and scale your applications, ensuring they run smoothly and efficiently in a production environment. In the next chapter, we'll explore more advanced deployment strategies, such as **Kubernetes** for container orchestration and **serverless architectures**.

www.ingramcontent.com/pod-product-compliance
Lightning Source LLC
LaVergne TN
LVHW022341060326
832902LV00022B/4169